A WEEKEND WARRIOR'S GUIDE TO

Expert Skiing

Introducing the innovative new SITS approach to skiing

STEPHEN PHIPPS WITH JUDY LIEDTKE

2nd Edition 2008

DaoEn Corporation
Boise, ID USA

A Weekend Warrior's Guide to Expert Skiing

Published by
DaoEn Corporation
P.O. Box 190136
Boise, ID 83719-0136

Visit our Web site at weekendwarriorsguide.com

DISCLAIMER:

This book is only for informational and educational purposes, and is not intended to give advice on skiing, exercising, or diet. The information in the book is intended for healthy adults age 18 and over. Skiing, exercise programs, and nutritional programs have always entailed a certain risk of injury, illness, or death. Always consult a doctor, exercise specialist, or health care professional before you begin any new exercise, nutrition, or skiing program or if you have questions about your health. The skiers and models pictured in this book are professionals and have had years of training and experience in the areas of skiing and exercising, including the use of the devices pictured. Like everyone who participates in sports and recreational activities, the readers of this book assume the risks and responsibilities inherent in skiing and other recreational pursuits referred to or mentioned in this book. This book is not a substitute for personal instruction in skiing.

Library of Congress Control Number: 2008933099
ISBN: 978-0-9789185-1-4

Technical Editor:	Todd Kelly
Ski Theory Editing:	Mark Kraley
Cover Design:	Bob Neal, Carton Sarton
Photo Credit:	Dee Childress
Photo Credit:	Elizabeth Espinoza
Photo Credit:	Bill Stephens
Cover Photo:	Adam Clark
Illustrations:	Craig Sarton with Neal/Gladselter

Manufactured in the United States of America

Printed on recycled, acid-free paper.

Acknowledgements

Special Thanks to the following:

Mark Kraley, Dan Kurdy, and Joey Cordeau; a great group of truly gifted skiers from Sun Valley, Idaho who helped teach and inspire us to become better skiers, and who volunteered their time whenever we called, to help us more accurately deliver the message of what it takes to be an expert skier.

Todd Kelly, a long-time friend and ski companion, not only edited this book, but tirelessly evaluated its content for accuracy; helping to further ensure this manuscript would be an excellent reference guide.

GIVE THEM SKIS AND SOME WILL FLY!
This maneuver represented cutting edge performance in the early 1970's. And today, this book is cutting a new edge with its introduction of the SITS© system of ski instruction.

CONTENTS

.

Part 3: SITS, Advanced Turn Dynamics for Every Type of Skiing

Part 4: SITS, The Other Tools

The Equipment Chain: You Are Only as Good as the Weakest Link

Bonus Section: Wait, There's More You Want to Know!

53-degree skiing is steeper than I remember.

Introduction

This is not a technical manual on how to ski. It is a book designed to give you some simple tools that will greatly enhance your ski experience. This book is not about tipping your skis on edge to facilitate endless skiing on groomed runs. It leaves that world behind, and teaches you how to use an energized ski for carving turns in any terrain.

Skiing is an individual endeavor and, like many activities, it includes the element of competition. In recreational skiing participants compete with themselves and their focus is internal, rather than directed at an opponent. Most skiers fantasize about becoming proficient enough to jet off into the steep and deep as easily as a duck takes to water, but the reality is far removed from this fantasy as the majority of skiers remain hopelessly trapped in the intermediate stage. There are three important reasons why most skiers throughout the world are hapless prisoners of boring runs. First, it is the desire to look good that makes skiers **Prisoners of the Groomed**. This desire keeps us from breaking out of the intermediate trap on our journey to becoming great skiers. The human ego is fragile, and it is difficult for us to step out of our comfort zones and risk looking bad, falling, or generally appearing like "hacks" on skis. Second, our fear of being put in an uncomfortable situation or even physically hurt keeps us from pushing our limits. Third, most skiers have never been exposed to an instructional method that is easy to understand and implement.

Well, it is time to take heart, as this book will give you the means to greatly improve your skiing techniques without you ever looking silly, feeling out of control, or facing significant fear. It will also allow you to do this without quitting you day job.

I think it is fair to say, most of us can be referred to as Weekend Warriors; trying to enjoy the world of outdoor skiing for a few precious weekends while escaping the realities of raising our families and earning a living. We understand completely that the weekend warrior does not have 80 or 90 days a year to devote to becoming an expert skier. That is exactly why we have spent many years developing an innovative new ski teaching method called the **Simple Imagery Teaching System™, or SITS™.** This learning method allows you to become a fabulous skier without devoting significant time and money to it, and you will still be able to keep up with your day-to-day responsibilities. It's a simple and effective approach to making you a better skier.

This system has been created with input from many sources, including the following: world champion skiers, professional ski instructors, alpine racers, freestyle competitors, and a few fanatical "techno" devotees of fundamentally perfect skiing technique.

This book provides you with a chance to be the skier you always wanted to be. It will take you on a journey of self-discovery and ultimately help you become a better skier, all the while having a great deal of fun and improving every single day.

Being an accomplished skier can bring a profound sense of satisfaction to many facets of your life by making you a more positive person, helping you feel better about the day-to-day grind of work, and teaching you that you can become very good at whatever you choose to engage in.

If you are like us, you spend time and money trying to understand the technical aspects of being a great skier, but all the terminology is too hard to understand and learning it is about as much fun as taking a class on statistics. My frustration with this scenario has led to the development of a new and better way of teaching skiing. SITS will have you skiing better the first day, and will ultimately help lead you to mastery of the crud, powder, moguls, and steeps. Become a student of SITS and your days of being an intermediate skier, merely surviving the skiing experience, will come to an end.

Until now, no one has been able to offer a truly simple explanation of the discipline of correct skiing: an approach so simple and taught in such a unique way you will have no trouble remembering what it is you should be doing on your journey to becoming an expert skier.

Throughout the evolution of modern ski technique there has been a plethora of terms that the average skier was never really able to understand or apply to their skiing. The list is long: heel thrust, counter-rotation, angulation, avalement, wedeln, Christiana Legere, reverse shoulder, and even the Dipsy Doodle from the 1930's. Admittedly, all these techniques have helped immensely to promote good skiing technique and improve the sport. They are the foundations upon which modern skiing is based, and most of these terms and techniques were developed by Olympic skiers or professional instructors. Still, it is a daunting task for the average skier to apply these technical breakthroughs to their skiing. Gone from this book are all the technical terms and complicated jargon. What remains is a great new approach to bringing out the expert skier in you.

The Simple Imagery Teaching System gives you a way to transform the essence of correct technique into action, using everyday images. We combine this imagery training with basic repetitive teaching drills directed at improving your skiing in a very short time. This cutting-edge teaching method employs the complex principles of kinesiology, body alignment, biomechanics, and development of the mind/body connection. But, because the SITS method has simplicity at its core you will not have to endure the academic and loathsome task of understanding and applying these terms. It has all been done for you and now the secrets of the complex and technical aspects of skiing are revealed in this new method. Everything has been compressed into an easy to understand system of teaching skiing.

SITS has four basic steps, applied in a specific order, which lead you toward becoming an accomplished skier. Our on-snow training techniques are designed to avoid making you look bad on the slopes, or put you in a training situation that is too difficult for you to handle. **In Part One,** SITS introduces you to simple imagery combined with the Visualize/Mimic/Evaluate (VME) assimilation exercise. This exercise is used for the first phase of engram development, a key component of becoming an expert skier. What's an engram you ask? At the most basic level, developing an engram can be described as creating a combined mental/physical memory of a movement, pose, or body position.

Technically speaking (and I promise to use the "T" word very sparingly), an engram is presumed to be an encoding in neural tissue that creates a persistence of memory linked to a subconscious record of physical movement. I know, that's a mouth full, but lucky for us, it is much easier to develop a specific engram than to understand the science behind it. Simply put, through engram development, your mind and body are able to memorize specific movement sequences and accurate body positions so that you don't have to think about it every time you do it. Essentially, you will have created an automatic movement pattern for your body during skiing. Throughout this book, the creation of engrams is made easy by imagery association, illustrated with common everyday objects, and then supplemented by simple training drills utilizing short term repetition. It is oh-so-easy to create engrams, as you will discover further into the book: nothing technical here.

First you will be shown how to create the mental portion of an engram through visualizing and mimicking the illustrations in this book. This will be accomplished through a series of off-snow learning exercises and can be done in the comfort of your home. To complete each section in Part One, you will be given additional on-snow drills that will focus on continuing the development of the complete engram for each body position.

In Part Two of the SITS method, you will learn the basics of a carved turn and continue to develop the physical portion of each engram using our unique approach to more on-snow training drills. This will complete the formation of the mind/body engrams that you will need to ski like an expert. For the moment, don't be concerned with completely understanding an engram and why it is an important component of advanced ski technique. You will develop a clear understanding of the term by the time you have completed the third phase of SITS.

During Part Three, you will continue to build on what you learned in Parts One and Two, as you develop an advanced understanding of a carved turn and then engage in a very different approach to skiing more advanced terrain.

Finishing up in Part Four, you will be motivated to stay the course until you have reached your goal of becoming a fantastic skier. You will learn about goal setting and motivational techniques designed to keep you focused and moving toward success, no matter how long it takes you.

This teaching method is designed to be easily usable by people just like you, eliminating the need to seek professional instruction in order to understand it.

We are excited about you joining us as we engage in this completely new and creative teaching method. Together we are going to start from scratch, and quickly show you how to transform yourself into an expert. Prepare to move away from traditional skiing methods and get ready to carve your turns on any terrain using proper body position and movement, rather than focusing solely on of using large muscles to steer or rotate your skis.

Concentrating on only large muscle utilization typically leads to a static body position, and leaves you fighting an ever skidding ski. We take a different approach to creating a turn, using a combination of imagery and continuous motion (throughout the turn). This does employ the large muscle groups, but only as a secondary subconscious function. You will learn to apply our creative imagery to correctly carve a turn based first on movement and secondly on applying a continuous and flowing force of the large muscles.

In the later chapters of the book, we bring you additional information on the "how to" of picking proper equipment, checking your body alignment, and tuning your skis in just five minutes. The very last section is unique to ski instruction books in that it addresses subject matter outside the teaching arena. In this section we will share with you tips on off-season training, ski specific strengthening exercises, and diet. In addition you will learn out secret approach to skiing unfamiliar resorts, and how we inexpensively ski Europe without even checking any baggage. No kidding!

With this book as your guide, you are about to enter the "Ski like a Pro" zone, becoming the envy of all your skiing buddies, and potentially, their guiding light to better skiing.

Using This Book

This book will provide you with all the tools needed to be the complete skier. It is not just a book of tips and tricks. It is a sequential learning process designed to take you from being a "doomed to the groomed" average skier up to an expert, in most, if not all conditions. The SITS (Simple Imagery Teaching System) method consists of four basic parts, and it is important you follow these steps in the order they are presented, and that you adhere to the training guidelines that accompany this teaching system. This approach will allow you to achieve your highest level of results.

The book is not intended to be read front to back in one sitting. Rather, it is intended that you "chunk it out" a section at a time. The simple techniques illustrated in this book are meant to be practiced individually to assure that you focus on only one core element at a time. After each element of ski technique has been practiced, it will be time to put it all together and ski like an expert.

Before beginning on-snow drills, study the *simple imagery* illustrations in **Part One** of the book. The illustrations show the correct body position necessary for advanced skiing. It is critically important to practice each position for a few minutes and to complete the mental imagery exercises. Do this in a quiet environment when you can find some time to be alone. Be sure to mimic each body position while standing in front of a mirror using the specific VME training method we outline in Part One.

Part Two will introduce you to the secrets of good pole plants and the basics of the carved turn using our CPCPU principle of turning. Again, this will be combined with simple imagery to add an unforgettable learning tool to your bag. It is imperative that you stay focused here and spend time doing the on-snow drills presented in this section. This will create the foundation for advanced carving and skiing difficult terrain.

Next, in **Part Three**, you will be given a relatively safe and relaxing way to put it all together and begin learning how to be a great powder, crud, bumps, and steeps skier. This will take you to **Part Four** of the system which will introduce you to the secrets of staying motivated to achieve your goal of becoming a great skier.

You will be happy to hear this book will help make you a better skier no matter what kind of skis you are using. But, I would like to make the point that you will progress more quickly, and have a lot more fun if you are skiing on the newest shape skis. Current model shape skis do make it easier to apply the techniques you will learn in this book. Ski technology is evolving at a significant rate every year and the newer your skis, the more likely they will perform well in a variety of conditions. With that said, if you want to have fun all over the mountain, you should choose an all-mountain ski and stay away from more race oriented models.

You can also do yourself a big favor by making sure you add modern boots and poles to your tool arsenal. When used in combination, newer ski, boot, and pole designs make it easier to successfully navigate a wider variety of challenging terrain. Just trust me on this one, but if you really want to know why current equipment is so great, see your local ski shop for details; just be sure to visit a specialty shop and not a big box retailer. Specialty shops usually have highly trained personnel on staff, many of whom have a vested interest in the store. You will also notice that the owners are almost always present in these smaller shops making for great customer service. Don't do yourself a disservice by doing all your research at the specialty store and then making your purchase at the "big box" in order to get a lower price. The access you will have to ongoing expertise in the specialty shop will be worth the few extra dollars.

I have written this book to be an all-inclusive instructional guide to expert skiing. Follow it closely and you will come out the other side having more fun on skis than you ever imagined possible.

Let's go for it!

Welcome to SITS: A Completely New Approach

The purpose of this book is to deliver a complete understanding of how to ski better, using a simple approach that will generate results quickly. To keep it simple, we use our breakthrough teaching method, SITS. This new teaching method is anything but traditional. It is an all encompassing approach that applies a combination of tools yet to be utilized as a total package by anybody in the ski industry. SITS (Simple Imagery Teaching System) gets you to the next level of skiing using a unique imagery based method of instruction, in combination with mental and physical engram development, easy practice drills, muscle relaxation techniques, and goal setting (to encourage continuing motivation to succeed).

For most people, the least familiar concept of this new method is engram development. Reiterating from this book's Introduction, an engram is presumed to be an encoding in neural tissue that creates a persistence of memory linked to a subconscious record of physical movement. Simply put, through engram development, your mind and body are able to memorize specific movement sequences and accurate body positions so that you don't have to think about it every time you do it. Really good news here – developing engrams is easy, and we give you a simple step-by-step process to ensure success so you can relax your way to better skiing.

You will become a better skier the very first day you use SITS, our four part teaching system that begins with the use of simple imagery to create insight into proper ski technique, and ends with safe and dynamic on-snow drills for skiing through the bumps, crud, powder, and steeps.

In Part One, you will learn that imagery development is one of the most powerful tools available for leading a person to the "aha" moment; turning simple images into discovery on skis. It has been said that awareness precedes meaningful choice, and with SITS you are able to quickly become aware of what it is your body should be doing to ski correctly. This is accomplished by showing you simple images or illustrations of everyday objects to create pictures in your mind that you can easily remember and take to the ski slopes. Once on the slopes, you will transform the images into actual body positions that will instantly begin to improve your skiing. Before you hit the slopes with your new body position images in mind, you will need to actually learn these positions. It is not enough just to imagine each position. To facilitate learning how your body should be positioned when skiing, we have developed the **VME (Visualize/Mimic/Evaluate)** training drill. VME incorporates a three step process beginning with an illustration. As you review the illustration, notice the general outline and every detail. Next place the illustration near a mirror that allows you to look in the mirror and view it at the same time. Now, with your eyes closed, visualize the shape precisely and then move your body into the position you have pictured in your mind. Without moving, open your eyes and evaluate your position compared to the illustration. This is the VME approach to beginning mental engram development. This simple exercise will allow you to start creating mental engrams of images in your subconscious, preparing you to practice good skiing techniques as you begin on-snow drills. The drills will help you convert the mental engrams you have learned into physical engrams. This enables you to replicate a technically correct ski stance without thinking about it as you carve turns down the slope.

Objects used to create our imagery for the SITS teaching method include: **a beach ball, a teacup, a common spring, balloons,** and other recognizable objects. This may sound weird to you, but just read the following examples and you will see the extraordinary value in using such objects to teach skiing.

In skiing, body relaxation starts with the hands, making it imperative that you grasp your poles with a relaxed grip exactly like holding a teacup. Think of a relaxed hand grip as starting the chain of relaxation in the body and preparing you to become an aggressive skier without using excess muscle tension or a static body position. Learning not to grab your pole grip tightly with all four fingers and your thumb is the first on snow drill you will need to do, requiring about 30 to 45 minutes for engram creation. This amount of time will actually allow you to make about 1000 pole plants using the correct grip. I would like to mention here that repetition is a major part of the secret to engram development.

In the next example, imagine you are holding your arms at chest height as if you are hugging a large beach ball (think 25-35 inch diameter, depending on your height and reach) and instantly, you have your arms correctly positioned for all types of skiing. Holding the beach ball against your chest illustrates the correct arm position when skiing; arms at chest level and wide apart, palms facing toward each other, and elbows held high. It's that simple! It is also easy to remember the beach ball imagery when you are on the slopes and working to position your arms like an expert.

After hands and arms, you will move on to proper head positioning, and so on, until every part of your body is reprogrammed. This assures you will come away from Part One with a complete image of the correct stance over your skis. This will give you the foundation necessary to begin training to ski like an expert.

Part Two will introduce you to the elusive carved turn, and a surefire way to learn it. Then we will hit the slopes and build on the imagery development from part one, giving you more on and off snow drills that enable you to learn carved turns, combined with proper edging technique. Remember these drills develop the physical engram for each correct movement and body position. They are designed to combine the previously studied images, now stored in your mind, with your muscle memory to finalize the formation of each mind/body engram. Completed engrams allow 2you to involuntarily perform the body movements necessary to ski like an expert.

Whoa! Is this starting to sound all too complicated? Fear not, there is good news, as it is all explained in this section using those *"everyday objects"* to illustrate proper body positions for edging and carving turns. This is combined with simple drills on and off snow to create the physical memory patterns. These drills are progressive, and each one must be mastered before you move on to the next engram drill.

Part Three builds on your learning from part two by supplying you with new information on how to create an advanced turn. We call it the RAT turn, which stands for *relaxed aggressive turn*, and introduces you to a carving technique developed through aggressive skiing, as apposed to tension based skiing. You will use your relaxed and correct body positions, combined with a new understanding of the carved turn, to put it all together and begin powering through turns aggressively on many different types of snow. Instruction will also include more advanced training on becoming a proficient skier in the crud, through the bumps, on the steeps, around the trees, and in the powder. In addition, we will give you the secrets to training for all these conditions. These training techniques utilize an approach that allows you to ski advanced slopes without experiencing fear, anxiety, or apprehension; all of which so frequently take front stage in our minds as we peer down a long steep, heavily bumped, or deep powder run. You will learn the tips, tactics and secrets that keep you out of trouble when skiing difficult terrain.

In Part Four you will gain the tools necessary to ensure you stay on track to becoming a great skier. We are going to share with you what it takes to stay motivated, create attainable goals, visualize success, and prepare for specific ski challenges.

Finally, to help put your skiing over the top we have included a *Bonus Section* where you will learn how to maintain and increase your ski conditioning during the off-season. This is achieved for you by utilizing ski specific dry land training activities that mimic the ski experience.

Come late fall, when you are ready to ski again, you will also be armed with progressive muscle relaxation techniques explained in this section. You will learn to prepare for any ski run you may choose to attempt. When you arrive at the moment of truth, standing above that legendary run, which has reduced so many skiers to a jumble of flailing arms and legs, you will be relaxed and able to completely focus on the daunting task in front of you. All of this creates the desired outcome of making you a well rounded, all mountain skier.

Keep in mind skipping ahead in the book is not the fastest route to becoming a better skier. Even if you think you have the basics of skiing under control, it is still best to do a review and make sure nothing is missed. Learning the fundamentals first is the only successful path to skiing a variety of conditions on any slope. When conditions are difficult even one weakness in your body position, technique, or equipment will reduce your descent from a euphoric experience to one of a fight for survival.

Developing Fundamentals Fast

CHAPTER 1

SITS: Imagery Development

For many centuries imagery has been used to help people understand how to do things better, and has been recognized as a way to help humans not only understand concepts, but also specific movements and body positions. Ballet has long engaged in the use of imagery for the development of body position and alignment, and even going back to Plato we see evidence of his understanding of imagery as an integral part of human development. In the *Phaedo*, Plato states that everything we can conceive of preexists as a so-called form or idea. I know that last thought is a bit removed from discussions about ski technique, but it does make the point that one of the greatest minds to ever exist supported the idea that imagery is a powerful part of our existence.

In this section, we will help you develop an understanding of the first chunk of the expert skiing skill set. You will become acquainted with all the imagery necessary to create a perfect stance in skiing, which is the first step toward empowering you to ski any terrain or snow condition. Chunking it out will help keep it manageable and provide you with a set of building blocks. By the end of the book all the blocks will be assembled, turning you into the complete skier.

The reason this happens is sort of mystical. In order for mind/body engram development to be completed, in part two you must first assimilate all the mental imagery created in part one into a total picture of what a correct stance on skis looks like. This picture should include, for example, where your hands and arms belong, what your head and shoulders are doing, how your legs are positioned, and the role of the core muscles of the stomach and back. Once you have this picture completed in your mind, it will be time to take it to the snow and teach your body, one part at a time, what position it should be in. The real fun starts on the snow as each drill, which targets a specific part of your body, has an immediate positive effect on your skiing. The other good news here is you need only concentrate on one body position at a time. Then you'll put it all together and start shredding the crud, bumps, powder, trees, and steeps; but not with reckless abandon. Control is the result of good ski technique.

CHAPTER 2

HANDS AND GRIP: How to Hold `Em and Use `Em

Until you understand what each major part of your body should be doing in a correctly executed ski turn, you certainly can't practice creating that turn! Throughout this section we will address each important part of the body that adds up to a correct ski stance and then it will be time to talk about carved turns.

It all starts here with the hands, then progresses through the arms, head, shoulders, torso, stomach, back, hips, legs, knees, ankles, and feet. Every part is important, but it just isn't that hard to learn how to coordinate all the parts. Combining all the parts into a perfect body position comes later. First I would like to address each area for you and share with you some imagery that will make it easy to understand how each body part should be positioned.

Teacup Grip

Starting with the hands, the most important thing to remember here is make sure those hands are always relaxed. ALWAYS RELAXED. Grab a ski pole out of the garage and pay attention to how you grip the pole. Be sure to imitate the exact grip used when skiing, and if you see every finger and your thumb wrapped around your pole grip (which is usually the case) you will need to change your hand position. A tight grip is a bad thing and can cause you to start using too much arm motion in your pole plant. This equates to added body movement and violates the first commandment of skiing: Always ski with a quiet upper body.

To correct this you need to think Tea Party. You significant other's mother has just invited the two of you to a Tea Party, and you will be going. Just a few things to remember: sit with your legs together, don't talk religion or politics, take out the tongue stud before you arrive (if applicable), and be sure to hold that tea cup correctly, *with your little finger and ring finger relaxed and pointing away from the cup handle*, while the thumb, index finger and middle finger are taking care of business by holding the tea cup in an upright position. Amazingly, this is exactly how you should also grip your pole. In the illustration Figure 2.1 you can see exactly how this grip should look to you. Notice that on the far left the hand is holding the teacup without help from the ring finger or the little finger. The middle illustration shows the same grip applied to a ski pole, and at the far right the incorrect hand grip is demonstrated.

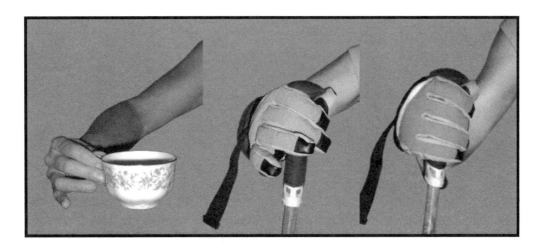

Figure 2.1 *The Teacup Grip. Your hand is gripping a ski pole correctly when the little finger and ring finger are relaxed and not resting against the grip. The gloved hand at the far right shows an incorrect grip, not relaxed and too forceful.*

The teacup grip allows you to relax not only your hands, but also your arms and shoulders. You don't believe me? Try placing you arms out in front of you just like you are holding onto your ski poles. Next close your hands tightly as if you are gripping your poles with all your fingers and your thumb. Squeeze your hands tight and then instantly relax your hands into the teacup grip. You will feel your arms and shoulders relax. This is the first step to relaxing your upper body which enables you to correctly respond to changing snow surfaces. When you are relaxed, it is much easier to maintain your balance and the upright stance required for expert skiing on changing terrain.

After you get your little finger to relax and let go, you need to think about placement of your hands, which should never be down by your hips or out of your sight. If you can always see your hands they are positioned correctly, meaning that they are placed wide apart, about chest high, and out in front of you.

Billy Kidd, the 1964 Olympic Silver Medalist in slalom, put it pretty succinctly in the 1998 February/March issue of Snow Country Magazine, *"If the hands are right, the body will be too"*.

SUMMARY

Hands have a relaxed hold on the pole, with the little finger and ring finger not exerting force on the pole grip.

VME TRAINING: HAND/GRIP INTERFACE

1. For this exercise you will need your ski poles
2. View and study every detail of the teacup series illustration 2.1.
3. Stand in front of mirror, with illustration Figure 2.1 near you.
4. Close your eyes, imagine your hands doing the teacup grip.
5. With eyes closed, pick up your ski poles and grip them.
6. Without moving, open eyes, compare your grip to the illustration.
7. Repeat this exercise until you can assume the position without thinking about it.

ON-SNOW TRAINING: Teacup Engram development

1. Pick a long groomed beginner or intermediate run.
2. Pause at the top of the run and review the teacup grip.
3. Before you begin the run flick your poles back and forth about 10 times making sure you have a relaxed grip on your pole, in the teacup position.
4. **Begin to ski, focusing *only* on the teacup grip.**

NEW INFORMATION!

5. *after each plant retract your pole by gently closing your hand, as you pull your elbow back and flick your wrist down.*
6. **After each retraction, return to the teacup grip for the next plant.**
7. **Make a minimum of four runs practicing only this open/close grip.**

This new hand grip on your pole may feel awkward at first, but soon it will become a natural part of your skiing.

CHAPTER 3

ARMS: Hold 'Em High and Wide

Beach Ball Arm Position

If you watch films of expert skiers ripping it up, you will notice that a large beach ball almost always will fit between their arms, and they will be holding it about chest high, with an erect upper body (not hunched over at the waist). This holds true regardless of the type of skiing or snow conditions.

If you have not spent a lot of time watching ski videos, you may not see this unless you play it in slow motion. Yeah I know, the beach ball won't always fit between their arms. But, look closely again and you will see that when their arms are out of position it is only a millisecond before they return them to the correct position, where both appendages are circumnavigating that imaginary beach ball at a chest high position. If you hold your arms at chest height as if you were grasping a large beach ball (think 25-35 inch diameter, depending on your height and reach) you now have your arms correctly positioned for all types of skiing. Again, holding the beach ball against your chest illustrates the correct arm position when skiing; with your arms at chest level and wide apart, your palms facing each other, and your elbows held high. It's that simple!

Figure 3.1 *Beach Ball Arms. Wrapping you arms around a large imaginary beach ball and holding it chest high will correctly position your arms for skiing. Your arms will be held wider than your body and your palms face each other.*

Your arms are correctly positioned when your elbows are about 9-11" wider than your body on each side.

Many practitioners of ski theory discount the importance of the arms in the overall picture of becoming a great skier. Don't think that for a single minute. Arms are one of, if not, the most important element of achieving a correct stance on skis. Do you know why? It's because a correct arm position keeps you centered over your skis. When you are leaning back on the tails of your skis or you are too far forward, your arms are always out of the "beach ball" position. If you are leaning back, your arms are probably held down by your waist and it won't be long before you can't see one or both of your hands. Once in this position on difficult terrain, you will fall. If you are bent forward on your skis your arms are most likely out in front, but too low and/or too close to your body.

Imagine you are skiing down the run and you are leaning back or bending forward over your skis. If you consciously and quickly return your hands to the beach ball position you will return to a centered position over your skis and you will also immediately stand taller on your skis. Both are very good things.

Turn Blocking

Keeping your arms in the beach ball position avoids *turn blocking*. If you allow an arm to come across your body while you are skiing, you are essentially blocking the next turn. To correct this situation you must move your arms back to the beach ball position before you can initiate the next turn.

This delay usually causes you to ski out of control or fall when on challenging terrain. Think of it this way: Skiing is about reacting to the ski run in a way that allows the skier to control their travel over irregular terrain. For this reason, it is important to realize how quickly things happen on skis. If you are going 20 miles per hour, you will travel 30 feet every second. At that rate you will descend a two mile long ski run in about six minutes. Obviously, even at this moderate speed, events happen in a hurry and it is imperative that you are able to react quickly to stay in control of the terrain. If the terrain controls you, you will be in for a bumpy ride; frantically trying to catch up with your skis.

Next time you are on the chairlift, spend some time watching other people ski and you will see many examples of people moving their arms across their bodies and blocking the next turn. Watch closely and you will see that they must first move their arm away from their body before initiating the turn. This works on intermediate groomed runs, but try this on a steep bump or crud run and you will be penalized immediately. In the following two photographs the skier is demonstrating an open body position and a closed body position. The skier with their hands in the beach ball position is instantly ready and will not have to make an arm adjustment before the next turn.

Beach Ball Arm Position   Arms blocking the next turn

Figure 3.2 *Turn Blocking: When your arms are in the correct position, you can quickly react to terrain changes, with no delay in setting up the next turn.*

Beach Balls and Bed Time Visualization

To help you complete the mental portion of the arm position engram try the following exercise. Right after you have retired to bed for the evening, relax and close your eyes while imagining you are skiing down an intermediate run. In your mind, picture yourself making slow relaxed turns with you arms in the beach ball position and your hands in the teacup grip as you hold your poles. Imagine making a few short runs before you fall asleep, focusing only on the arm position and the hand grip. This should consume about five or ten minutes. Repeat the exercise in the morning before you get out of bed. The first few times you do this it may seem difficult, but with practice you will become proficient at this exercise.

Don't try to visualize other parts of your body, just create a rhythm while holding your arms high and wide, and flicking your wrists back and forth to make imaginary pole plants before each turn. Continue this exercise until you add the next body position discussed in this section. If you are progressing quickly, you may only need to do each visualization for several nights. Engram development is less effective if you skip ahead and start doing the more involved visualization exercises, as would be the case if you were visualizing the entire body stance before practicing this segment. It is widely

26

believed that any visualization learning experience is enhanced if it is the last thing you think of before sleeping, and the first thing you think of right after you wake for the day.

CUMULATIVE SUMMARY: Pole Grip combined with Arm Position

1. Hands have a relaxed hold on the pole, with the little finger and index finger not exerting force on the pole grip.

NEW INFORMATION

2. Arms are held high and wide, as if gripping a beach ball at chest level.
3. Palms are facing each other.

VME TRAINING: Beach ball arms and teacup grip

1. View and study every detail of the Beach Ball illustration Figure 3.1, page 24.
2. Stand in front of the mirror, with the illustration in sight.
3. Close your eyes, imagine your arms grasping a large beach ball, chest high.
4. With your eyes still closed, actually move your arms into position.
5. Without moving, open your eyes, compare your position to Figure 3.1.
6. Study the illustration carefully, making sure you are mimicking it exactly as it appears.
7. Repeat this exercise until you can assume the position without thinking about it.

As you practice this new arm position you may feel awkward and suspect you look stupid. You don't; you look like an expert!

POLE PLANT TIP: THE FLICK, STAB, AND RELEASE

Now that you have learned the teacup grip and beach ball arms, it is time to think about the entire pole plant. We refer to it as the flick, stab, and release.

1. To initiate the plant, flick your pole out toward the tip of your ski using mostly an upward motion of the wrist.

2. With a slight extension of the elbow, stab the pole into the snow.

3. Slightly retract the elbow and cock the wrist upward to reset for the next plant.

The complete pole plant is covered in more detail, starting on page 48.

28

CHAPTER 4

HEAD POSITION: Up, With Eyes Looking Ahead

Your head needs to be up with your eyes looking forward when you are holding the imaginary beach ball chest high. Be sure to look out in front of you, and never down at your skis. Keeping your head up in skiing allows you to see what is coming and prepare for it. It also helps you maintain an upright position in your upper body. To do this imagine that your arms, shoulders, and head are continually floating up. Your head becomes a balloon filled with helium, while other helium-filled balloons push up on your arms. To help ingrain this in your mind, place your arms at your sides. Now imagine the balloons starting to lift them into the beach ball position, and simultaneously, your head (as a balloon) lifts up, elongating your spine. Feel how light you become as your spine extends upward, your arms float up, and your head is floating toward the sky. When your head is filled with helium (metaphorically speaking) it will never be able to look down at your skis. Guys, sneak into the bathroom, close the door and pretend you are ballet dancers. Float up on your toes as you lift you arms and head. Begin to think of this as part of the dance your upper body will do on skis. Gals, you are luckier, and can do this in sight of everyone without feeling insecure.

When skiing, keep your head up and arms high, with your eyes looking ahead, **LIKE A BALLET DANCER**. All great skiers assume this position.

Figure 4.1 *Floating Upper Body. Think about your head and arms floating up as you look ahead down the slope.*

CUMULATIVE SUMMARY: Hands, Arms, Head, and Eyes

1. Hands have a relaxed hold on the ski pole, with the little finger and ring finger not exerting force on the pole grip.
2. Arms are held high and wide, as if gripping a beach ball at chest level.
3. Palms are facing each other.

NEW INFORMATION

4. Head is held up with the eyes looking ahead rather than down at your skis.
5. You are standing with your upper body erect.

VME TRAINING: Hands, Arms, Head

1. View and study every detail of the Floating Upper Body illustration (fig. 4.1).
2. Stand in front of the mirror with the illustration in view.
3. Close your eyes; imagine your head floating straight up like a balloon.
4. Also imagine your arms floating up into the beach ball position.
5. Without moving, open your eyes and compare your position to illustration 4.1.
6. Make sure your head is up and your eyes are looking ahead, not down.

ON-SNOW DRILL: Head Floating Up Engram Development with Beach ball and Teacup.

1. Pick a long, groomed beginner or intermediate run.
2. Pause at the top of the run to review your arm, hand, and head positions.
3. Begin to ski, this time focusing only on your head and arms floating.
4. As your head and arms float, the arms should be chest high and wide, and your eyes should be looking ahead, not down at your skis.
5. Make a minimum of four practice runs.

CHAPTER 5

TORSO: Shoulder, Chest, Stomach, and Back

Your upper body has two very important assignments to fulfill as you ski like an expert.

First, your upper body is most effective when it remains quiet, erect, and adjusted to the pitch or steepness of the hill as it relates to your direction of travel. This means your upper body should always be perpendicular to the slope angle you are descending. It is important to realize that the slope of the hill is not always the same as the fall line. To better understand this think about the difference between skiing straight down the hill and skiing at a downward angle across the hill. These two directions of travel represent different slope angles, and you need to keep your chest facing the direction of travel at all times. This allows your upper body to be correctly positioned so that it can also remain perpendicular to the direction of travel.

You should not be rotating your shoulders back and forth, swinging your arms across your body, or bending your upper body significantly forward. For our purpose, quiet means lack of movement in the upper body. Relax and sssh!

Figure 5.1 *Body Perpendicular to the Slope. The skier on the left is skiing in the proverbial back seat and does not have control over the front of the skis. The skier on the right is skiing with the body perpendicular to the slope. The slope and the body form a 90 degree angle. To better understand this concept think of your upper body always being perpendicular to the direction of travel regardless of whether you are skiing directly down the fall line or not. In the drawing on the right, the angle of the skier's back and lower legs match.*

31

Secondly, the chest must be squared off to the angle of descent. For the purpose of this discussion, let's now assume you are skiing directly down the fall line. To visualize this position, imagine your shoulders and chest are always facing downhill, and by this I mean directly down the fall line. To understand where the fall line is, look down the slope and imagine a smooth skiing surface upon which you release a soccer ball. The soccer ball will always roll straight down the fall line, for that is the nature of gravity. If the slope slants down and off to the right, the ball will always roll down and to the right, exactly following the fall line (or shall we say roll line?). Remember we are talking about two slope angles here, the angle down and the angle to the side. The ball will find its path down the run in direct correlation to the steepest of the two angles. A run that slopes off to one side or the other is referred to as having an off-angle or off-camber fall line.

Conversely, if a run has a perfect fall line there will only be one angle of descent and the ball will always roll right down the middle of the run until it reaches the bottom. This type of run does not slope to the right or left as you descend it.

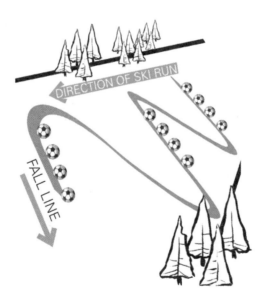

Figure 5.2 *Soccer Ball Will Always Find the True Fall Line. In this example the Zigzag line shows a fall line descent down a run that slopes off to the skier's left. You can use ski traverses to always stay in the fall line on off-angle slopes. The soccer balls illustrate the path you would descend. Begin by skiing to the bottom side of the run, then traverse back to top side of run; repeating this sequence until you reach the bottom.*

Expert skiers most often descend a slope skiing directly down the fall line. So, always keep your chest facing toward the true fall line when descending down it. If, however, you are skiing back and forth across the fall line you are still going down hill at some specific angle of descent. Just remember to apply the same concept as you do when skiing the fall line; keep your body perpendicular to the direction of travel (downward descent angle).

The real problems start when you move your shoulders out of the fall line (or direction of travel) and rotate them to the left or right. The deal here is that gravity is always pulling you down the fall line, and you can choose to face it or rotate away from it. Imagine trying to ski down the fall line with your shoulders facing away from it. This is very difficult to do, and except for stunt skiers, this inevitably ends in a fall or you must stop. Think of it as twisting out of the fall line with you upper body, while your legs are still going in the direction of the gravitational pull. You will be all twisted up with no where to go, except off your skis.

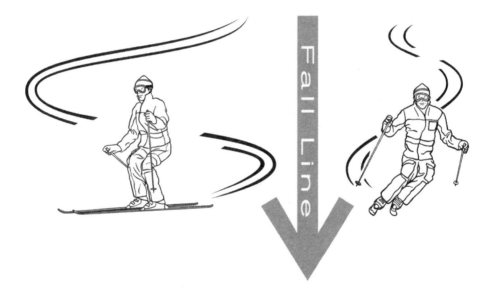

Figure 5.3 *Facing the Direction of Travel. The upper body of the skier on the left is not facing down the fall line, and he will be unable to turn where he wants to. Notice he has dropped his right hand, causing his right shoulder to rotate uphill and pull his upper body out of the fall line. The skier on the right has her upper body facing the direction of travel, down the fall line, and she can turn when and where she chooses. Her arms are in the beach ball position.*

As you ski, if your upper body moves unnecessarily, it creates momentum; always in the wrong direction. To illustrate the importance of keeping your upper body quiet when skiing imagine trying to slow or even alter the course of a ten pound brick (probably weighing less than your head), while it is hurdling through space. I don't pretend to be an expert on the forces exerted by flying objects, but even if it is only traveling ten miles per hour, it would certainly knock you down. Now, imagine this ten pound brick is your head and it starts moving, with your shoulders, in a direction opposed to your skis. You will not be able to stop this upper body momentum in time to place your next turn where you intend it to be. Again, you will have arrived at the point where the terrain is controlling you. This illustrates the importance of keeping your upper body quiet. I use this moving head scenario to help you understand how much force is generated when you start moving or twisting your upper body too much while skiing down the fall line.

When the going gets tough, it has been said that the plight of the intermediate skier is to forever traverse the fall line. However, this book will give you the tools needed to learn how to expertly ski the fall line in absolute control on any slope.

Ok, now we all understand how important the shoulders, chest, and head are to skiing, and that these body parts always need to be quietly pointed downhill. Add to this a tight stomach, held flat against your lower back, and you have the makings of a great upper body – for skiing.

The lower back and stomach actually enable the spine to be positioned correctly. For the purpose of expert skiing, your lower back must be a bit rounded. This is best demonstrated by standing up and pulling your stomach in tight, and flat against your back. When you do this you will feel your hips align themselves forward. You have just discovered a fundamental element of good skiing, the hips forward position. Coming up in the "Lower Body" section we will give you an illustration and VME exercise to teach you just how far forward your hips should be when skiing. But, for now let's continue our discussion of the upper body position.

There is one more important point to make about the shoulders that ties into skiing with a slightly rounded lower back. To compliment the correct lower back position you should relax your shoulders just a little by allowing them to slump forward ever so slightly. When studying Figure 5.5 on page 37 you will see the shoulders are relaxed a bit forward and the forward lean of the lower spine actually matches the forward lean of the lower leg.

Figure 5.4 *Upper Body Position.* *The skier on the left is bending too far forward at the waist, while the skier at the far right drops the butt behind the feet. Only the center skier is positioned correctly over the skis. The lower back is relaxed and round, with the shoulders slightly slumped forward and the entire upper body is centered over the skis*

Next time you're skiing concentrate on minimizing upper body movement. This will help you ski down the hill without disrupting the lower body. Make sense? Think of it this way; when the upper body mass moves significantly in any direction there must be a reaction or adjustment by the lower body to counter this movement. To demonstrate it, try standing with your feet together and legs locked in a straight up position as you move your upper body. If you move your chest just 15 to 20 inches in any direction your lower body also must move or you will fall.

35

CUMULATIVE SUMMARY: Hands, Arms, and Upper Body

1. Hands have a relaxed hold on the ski pole, with the little finger and index finger not exerting force on the pole grip.
2. Arms are held high and wide, as if gripping a beach ball at chest level.
3. Palms are facing each other.
4. Head is held up.
5. Eyes are looking ahead, and not down at skis.
6. Upper body is erect, quiet, and perpendicular to the slope.

NEW INFORMATION

7. Shoulders and chest are facing down the fall line.
8. Tight stomach, held against lower back.
9. Round or curve your lower back toward ski tips. Do not bend your entire body forward.

VME TRAINING – Upper Body Position

1. View and study every detail of the upper body position illustration 5.5, page 37.
2. Stand with the side of your body visible in the mirror and the illustration within sight.
3. Close your eyes; imagine you are standing at the top of a ski run.
4. Lift your arms to the beach ball position; assume the teacup grip
5. With eyes still closed, imagine you are looking ahead and lightly tighten your abdominal muscles.
6. Now round your lower back, causing it to curve forward. Hold this position.
7. Flex ankles forward, and hold to complete the position.

Without moving, open your eyes and compare your position to the illustration.

ON-SNOW DRILL: Developing the Upper Body Engram

1. Begin by locating a long beginner or intermediate run, not a cat track.
2. Pause at the top of the run to review the correct upper body position.
3. As you ski two runs, focus on a quiet upper body and rounded lower back.
4. On run three make sure your shoulders are hunched very slightly forward.
5. As always, use the beach ball arm position and the tea cup grip.
6. To finish this session make four runs putting it all together with:
    a. Beach ball arms.
    b. Teacup grip.
    c. Rounded lower back.
    d. Quiet upper body facing down the hill.
    e. Body does not rotate out of the fall line.

Figure 5.5 *Correct Body Position. The skier is looking ahead and has relaxed shoulders with a good arm position. The angle of the lower legs matches the angle of the lower back. That's a good thing!*

As you practice these positions you may feel awkward and suspect you look stupid. You don't, and for the first time you do look like an expert! How you think you look and how you actually look are rarely the same. Don't believe us? We strongly recommend you make a video of yourself skiing. It is a great learning tool.

During the video make a run skiing just like you always have, and then make a run skiing with your arms in the beach ball position while keeping your upper body still. You be the judge when deciding which style looks more like an expert.

CHAPTER 6

LOWER BODY: Hips, Legs, Knees, and Feet

The lower body plays the roll of the A Team when you are skiing like an expert. The upper body is responsible for staying quiet and planting the poles, while it is the lower body's very important assignment to turn those skis. The first step is to make sure the lower body is free from physical deterrents that inhibit it from turning correctly. Almost everyone has at least one physical inhibitor that can adversely effect their skiing. If you truly want to ski like an expert it is imperative you get a boot alignment assessment.

PHYSICAL INHIBITORS MAKE SKIING DIFFICULT

We recommend every skier have a boot alignment assessment performed by a specialist. Do not confuse this with custom boot fitting. Boot alignment goes much further, as the goal of a good alignment is to perfect your stance over your skis. It assures you are balanced over your skis allowing you to shift your weight from ski to ski without engaging in compensating or corrective movements. When properly aligned, a skier's lower body parts maintain a cohesive biomechanical relationship. An accurately aligned lower body has the hips, knees, lower legs, ankles, and feet stacked on top of ski boots so that everything is positioned to work together effectively.

A misaligned lower body can wreak havoc on your skiing, causing a variety of problems such as pain, premature fatigue, unnecessary body movement, and in some cases even injury. Chapter 23 is dedicated solely to alignment and will give you a clear understanding of everything involved in having an alignment specialist correct any lower body incongruence you may have.

Most ski or boot specialty shops can help you with this procedure, or direct you to a boot alignment specialist. As previously mentioned, this subject is covered in depth in Chapter 23 of this book, and yes this is the one and only time we feel it is acceptable to jump ahead, because good skiing starts with a properly aligned body.

Understanding how the aligned lower body is positioned is the first step to creating a properly carved turn. The lower body must always be centered over your feet with the hips between your heels and your toes. Actually, your entire body should be *centered fore and aft over your skis* in this manner at all times. Now that I have said that, forget about your entire body being centered over your skis, and let's talk about your lower half being centered over your *feet*. Visualize yourself standing up straight, and then imagine a vertical line running parallel to your body from the front edge of your foot up past your head. Now add another line running from your heels, up past your head still parallel to your body. Add one more line to your image that runs up through your body exactly centered between the other two lines. This third line runs through the center of your hips, if your hips are correctly positioned between your heels and your toes. Illustration 6.1 shows the correct position of your hips if you are centered over your feet, which by the way, ends up centering your entire body mass over your skis.

Figure 6.1 *Hips are always centered over the feet.* **The skier on the left is standing with the hips centered over the feet. The skier on the right is skiing with the hips centered over the feet.**

With your hips centered over your feet you are positioned correctly as your ankles flex forward, and your legs bend at the knee during a carved turn.

When you are centered over your feet, your skis are less likely to jet out ahead of you in the turn. Flexing your ankle to press your lower leg forward to the front of your boot will help you stay centered over your skis. This pressing force can vary throughout the ski turn as we will explain in "Basics of the Carved Turn" in Part Two. If you are not centered over your feet during the turn, your skis will generally accelerate faster than you, and you will come out of the turn with your body behind your skis – Not Good!

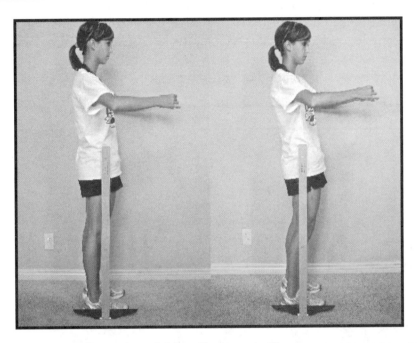

Figure 6.2 Check for natural hip alignment. *To understand how your hips line up over your feet you can do this simple T-square test. It will help you feel how much you need to move your hips fore or aft to center them over your feet. In the left picture the model is standing naturally. In the right picture she has pushed her hips forward about three inches to get them centered over her feet. To ski correctly, your hips must remain centered over your feet even as your stance changes from upright to flexed at the ankles.*

As you can see in Figure 6.2 the photo on the right shows the hips centered over the feet. This is where the hips need to remain all the time when skiing. From this point, whenever we say bend your knees, we are really saying *flex your ankles* forward to bend your knees. This is a very important point because if you do not flex your ankles, you must drop your butt to bend your knees. This is a big no-no in ski technique, as dropping your butt pulls your hips back behind your feet and you are no longer centered over your skis. No one can ski like an expert with their butt hanging out behind them. In Figure 6.3 you can clearly see the difference between flexing your ankles to bend your knees, and dropping your butt to bend your knees. By flexing your ankles you can always keep your hips centered over your feet. Choose a ski boot that will allow you to flex your ankles forward, but make sure your boot is very stiff laterally. Racers can benefit from extremely stiff boots, while a boot that is easy to flex forward is better for the recreational skier. You save a significant amount of energy in the course of a day's skiing if you don't have to continually push strongly into your boots for turn initiation. Many skiers will not be able to flex stiff boots enough to ski correctly, thus making a pretty strong case for staying away from high performance race boots. If you are a serious racer please disregard that last statement.

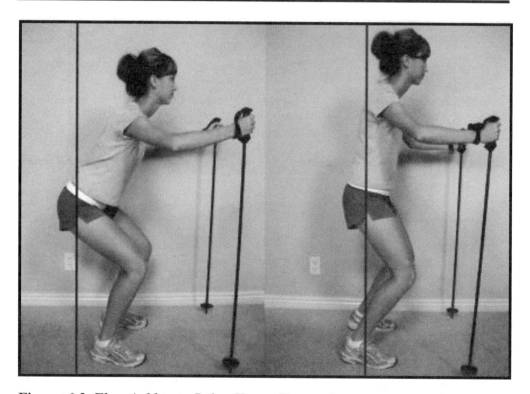

Figure 6.3 *Flex Ankles to Drive Knees Forward. The picture on the left shows knees flexed by dropping the butt. This places the hips behind the feet (incorrect). The picture on the right shows the ankles flexing forward to allow the hips to stay centered over the knee (correct).*

CUMULATIVE SUMMARY: Upper Body and Lower Body.

1. Hands have a relaxed hold on the ski pole, with the little finger and index finger not exerting force on the pole grip.
2. Arms are held high and wide, as if gripping a beach ball at chest level.
3. Palms are facing each other.
4. Head is held up.
5. Eyes are looking ahead, and not down at skis.
6. Upper body is erect, quiet, and perpendicular to the slope.
7. Shoulders and chest are facing down the fall line.
8. Tight stomach, held against lower back.
9. Round or curve your lower back toward ski tips.

NEW INFORMATION

10. Hips are pushed forward using the butt muscles.
11. Ankles flex forward to facilitate the knees bending forward as well.
12. Your legs are in a neutral position between the front and rear of your boot cuff.

This allows your legs to move forward and backward. But, the caveat here is never to allow the back of legs to touch the back of your boot cuff for more than an instant.

VME TRAINING: Lower Body Position

1. Study the right side of the photo illustration 6.3 on page 42, and then place it within sight of your mirror.
2. Stand in front of the mirror so you can see a side view of your body.
3. Close your eyes and imagine you are standing at the top of a ski run.
4. Place your arms out in front of you for balance.
5. With eyes closed and your feet flat on floor, push your knees forward.
6. Flex your butt muscles and move your hips forward until they are centered over your feet.
7. Without moving, open your eyes to compare your position to the illustration.

ON-SNOW DRILL: Developing the Lower Body Engram

1. Begin by locating a long groomed beginner or intermediate run.
2. Pause at the top of the run to review the correct lower body position.
3. Before you start to ski, repeatedly drive your hips forward. Accomplish this by flexing your ankles forward to bend your knees until hips are centered over your feet.
4. Begin skiing, focusing only on hip placement.
5. Continue to feel your hips pushing forward *(you should feel increased pressure on the balls of your feet)*.
6. For most people this means pushing your hips forward by flexing your ankles and tightening the butt muscles.
7. During this exercise be sure to make slow speed turns on easy terrain.

FINAL LIST- PART ONE: Elements of the Correct Body Position

1. Hands use the teacup grip.
2. Arms are in the beach ball position.
3. Balloon Head is floating up, with eyes looking out and down the hill.
4. Upper body is erect and perpendicular to the slope angle of the hill.
5. Stomach is tight and held against your back (not really, just feels like it).
6. Lower back is rounded.
7. Shoulders are slightly relaxed forward.
8. Hips centered over feet, between your heels and toes.
9. Ankles are flexed forward to create a slight forward bend in the knee.

Note: After you have practiced each position one at a time, you can move up to focusing on two or three per ski run. To cover the entire list, always make at least three runs.

44

PART ONE SUMMARY

- Most skiers grip their poles too tightly and this causes their upper body to be tense, rather than relaxed. ***Use the teacup grip to correct this problem.***

- If your arms are not held high, wide, and out in front of you, then you will always be late to the party (or turn). Put another way, the terrain will always be controlling you, instead of the other way around. When your arms are held incorrectly you must always move them into the correct position before you can initiate your next turn. In challenging terrain you do not have time for this maneuver. Everything happens too fast! ***Keeping your arms in the beach ball position moves your skiing experience from reactive to proactive.***

- Keep your head up when you ski. If you are looking at your skis, you will not be able to see the ever changing landscape and snow conditions. ***Keeping your head up enables you to see terrain changes and make adjustments.***

- A lot of people allow their upper body to wreak havoc on their skiing style. Holding you stomach tight and flat against your back helps keep your upper body motionless. ***Keeping your upper body quiet and your chest pointing down the slope allows your lower body to make turns without interruption.***

- The lower body performs wonderfully for you if your hips remain centered between your heels and your toes. To do this, flex your ankles forward and your shin will move into the front of the boot tongue with the knees following. ***By flexing your ankles your shins are always pressed lightly against the front of your boots. Your hips need to be tucked forward and held in place by flexing of the butt muscles. Then you will be centered over your feet and skis.***

- To reinforce your first phase of the engram learning experience review the simple imagery presented in this section. ***Using VME, remembering to practice your body positions on a regular schedule before you going skiing.***

- More practice makes perfect, and we all like it when it is easy like this. Review the bed time visualization exercise on page 22, except now close your eyes and see your whole body skiing down a low angle groomed run. That's easy. *Be sure to do five consecutive days of the bed time visualization exercise for your entire body.*

SITS: Creating On-Snow Mind/Body Engrams

CHAPTER 7

CORRECT POLE USE: Creating the Perfect Plant

Every expert skier uses an expert pole plant on every turn. Why? Because the proper use of poles is an extremely important part of being a great skier. Pole use, combined with how tightly you hold them, has a major influence on your skiing. Use a pole wrong and your upper body will never be in position to allow your lower body to stay centered over your skis.

Next time you are riding a chairlift observe different skiers as they plant their poles. You will see a variety of styles, most of which are wrong. There is the double pole plant, the one-sided pole plant, the late pole plant, the non-existent pole plant, the across the body pole plant, the row boat pole plant, and my favorite, the knock-the-gates-out-of-the-way pole plant. You know, the one where a skier swings their arms from side to side as if to knock imaginary race gate poles out of their path.

To determine if you are using your poles correctly have a friend positioned about 75 to 100 yards directly below you on the ski run. As you ski down to your friend, have him observe your pole plants. If your friend cannot see eight to twelve inches of light between your pole shafts (or elbows) and the sides of your body at all times, then you need to make an adjustment to your pole plant technique. This is easy to do by making sure your arms are always held chest high and wide, with your hand utilizing the teacup grip to hold your poles. The teacup grip allows you to flick your pole back and forth using only your wrist. This helps keep your arms quiet and in the correct position.

Your entire body is an interconnected string of muscles and joints, and every time you move one part of your body another part must also move, rotate, or somehow change position. For skiers, this means too much upper body movement forces the lower body out of position, making skiing correctly difficult, if not impossible.

An effective pole plant occurs at the end *not the beginning* of each turn. Don't initiate your turn and then plant your pole. To determine if your pole plant is timed correctly, have a friend stand down the hill while watching you make a series of turns on groomed run. If you are observed planting after you begin each turn ask your friend for a little more help. Pick a nice gentle slope and have the friend *follow behind* you as you ski down the hill. Your partner will shout out the word "plant" as you are finishing each turn. This will help you speed up your pole plants as you learn to use them to set up the next turn. Also be sure to make your pole plants deliberate, yet quick. Think of each plant as *a flick, stab, and release* sequence.

With the teacup grip you are able to *flick* the tip of the pole forward toward your next plant. When skiing directly down the fall line, a good rule of thumb is to always plant your pole at the tip of your ski. The *stab* occurs when you extend your elbow until the tip contacts the snow. To make sure your pole plants remain fluid from turn to turn, always *release* the plant quickly. This may be accomplished by a slight recoil of the elbow. Gently close your hand around the grip when returning your pole from the plant to the ready position. Resume the teacup grip as you flick the pole out toward the next plant. The hand is **opening** on the *flick* and **closing** on the *release,* or return phase of the plant.

THERE SHOULD NEVER BE ANY SIDE-TO-SIDE ARM MOVEMENT ACROSS YOUR BODY AS YOU SKI!

Figure 7.1 *Powder skiing with correct arm and hand placement. Using the teacup grip, Mark Kraley flicks his left pole toward the next plant, as he floats through the virgin snow at Soldier Mountain in Idaho. His right hand has gently closed to return his right pole to the ready position.*

Lastly, you will need to think about the type and length of your poles. It is generally accepted that the only consideration when buying ski poles is the length. Not true! The type of grip, the grip offset, and the pole swing weight are also very important. These elements of pole design and style are discussed later in chapter 25 on pages 193 and 194. For now we will limit this discussion to pole length.

To determine the correct pole length, you will need to visit your local ski shop. Place a ski pole upside down with the basket resting on top of your fist and against your thumb. Bend slightly at the knee, as if in a skiing stance and place the pole grip on the floor just in front of your feet. Make sure the pole shaft is straight up and down as you observe the angle created by your upper arm and forearm. This angle should be ninety degrees with your forearm parallel to the floor. Because shoe heel height can vary from ½ to 4 inches, I suggest you do this pole measurement while wearing ski boots. Do not do it with bare feet.

Using this method to determine pole length will get you very close to the correct length. You can make more precise adjustments to your pole length by making some on-snow observations about your skiing style.

If your poles are too long it may be difficult to swing them. You may drag your poles a lot, and in the bumps you will be jamming them into bumps repeatedly. Long poles also can cause you to stand too tall and interfere with your ability to move your body through a cleanly carved turn. If your poles are too short you may ski with a hunched over upper body. A short pole will also cause you to reach out too much to contact the snow resulting in a bizarre skiing style. None of us want that.

When buying longer poles or cutting your current set down, be sure to proceed with caution. You know the saying: Measure twice and cut once. To apply this logic to ski poles try renting a pair that is closer to the correct length. If this is not convenient, make small rather than large adjustments. We have been through this process and discovered that ½ inch can be a big change. Good luck with it.

KEY POINTS FOR CORRECT POLE USE

1. Hold arms at chest level and wide, with hands using the teacup grip.
2. Use only the wrist to flick the pole from plant to plant.
3. The pole tip always leads the pole to the next plant.
4. Plant pole tip out at the tip of the ski, creating the correct angle down hill.
4. Do not drive your hand forward; instead think of it as swinging the pole tip.
5. Extend your elbow out until the tip contacts the snow.
6. Close fingers around grip and retract elbow to swing pole back from the plant.

CHAPTER 8

BASICS OF THE CARVED TURN: Introducing CPCPU

It is *almost* time to hit the slopes again and convert your newly learned mind/body engrams (body positions), into correctly carved turns. But first, I am guessing you will enjoy a little discussion on how a carved turn actually happens on snow. As you read through this dissertation on carving, always imagine the carving is taking place on a nicely groomed and very smooth intermediate run. This is the kind of run that allows you to relax and float euphorically down the slopes.

In the SITS method your lower body creates a ski turn using a four part continuous movement sequence referred to as: *Compress, Point, Continuous Push, and Up* (CPCPU). Say what? Well, all I am saying is this is the perfect lead-in to the next phase of the SITS system. In this section of Part Two, we begin with an explanation of the basic carved turn utilizing the CPCPU turn dynamics. Once again, it is really simple and clearly illustrated by an everyday object; the common spring.

Figure 8.1 *Compressing Springs to Start the Turn. From an upright stance compress the imaginary springs forward with your knees. Next, point your knees in the direction of the turn. Keep pressure on the springs throughout the entire turn.*

The essence of the carved turn is found in getting your skis tipped up on their edges. Have you ever wondered what exactly is happening here? Let me start this discussion by saying I will not answer this question with a laundry list outlining some complicated series of steps required in an exact order to get the desired result of a single carved turn.

I will share with you the few elements necessary to accomplish a rhythmic dance of coordinated and balanced turns down the ski slope. As we dissect the components of the carved turn I want you to promise me you will remember to always think of a ski turn as much more than a sum of parts. I want you to think of the carved turn as a fluid continuous flowing motion. A motion that takes you down, around, and up again. That's it, the basic carved turn! Think of the down part, or initial phase of a turn as using your knees to compress two strong springs that are hooked to your knees and extend out to the tips of your skis. This is phase one of the carved turn, and this compression action is identified by **C** in the **CPCPU** turn sequence.

The compressing action loads your skis with energy as they push against the snow. Creating this load on your skis causes them to counter flex. To see this, next time you are in the local ski shop lay one of their skis on a flat hard surface. You will see that the ski bows up in the middle, while only the tips and tails are touching the surface. Push down on the center of the ski until it touches the surface, and then release your hand quickly. The ski springs upward a bit as it releases the energy you loaded onto it. When skiing, you compress the imaginary springs and the ski flexes counter to its natural shape due to the pressure you are exerting on it. When you press on the ski during an actual turn it will *counter flex* a great deal, substantially increasing the energy you load into it. Later, we will discuss using this energy to correctly finish the turn.

In the second phase of your turn, you continue to apply pressure to the imaginary springs and point your knees in the direction you want to go. This pointing action, which drives your knees into the turn initiates the edging of your skis. **P**ointing your knees is the second phase of a carved turn and it is identified by the **P** in CPCPU. The key point to remember when carving good turns is to make sure you keep the above mentioned springs compressed *throughout the entire turn*. Simply keep pressure on the front of your skis by continuously pushing on the springs. Compressing in the beginning and then letting up before you are through the turn is a common mistake of immediate skiers, and even advanced skiers make this mistake too often. Applying pressure to the front of your skis by **C**ontinuously **P**ushing on the imaginary springs throughout the turn is identified by the second **CP** in CPCPU.

If you let up on those imaginary springs, the skis can accelerate out ahead of you, and now you are playing catch up. Guess what? If you are trying to play catch up in challenging terrain you will quickly learn it is not only difficult to accomplish, but that it rarely ends with you in control and centered back over your skis. So let's avoid it and continuously push our knees forward through the entire turn. Most intermediate skiers fail here because they are not patient enough.

The Art of Pressure Control

Being able to decrease or increase the pressure on your skis will help you control the size and shape of your turn. Continuously pressing on your imaginary springs throughout the turn pressures the skis, causing them to counter flex. Counter flexing a ski loads it with energy which can be used to control your turn. The subtle variations in the amount of pressure you exert on your skis determine the quickness and shape of your turns. This can be likened to driving a car on a snow covered road. When you brake, the car responds according to the amount of pressure you apply to the pedal. If you apply a lot of pressure quickly the ride can get exciting, yet if you apply just a small amount of pressure the car will react more predictably. Suffice it to say this is applicable to skiing as well. Press hard on your imaginary springs and your skis react quickly and forcefully. Press lightly on your skis and your turns will develop more gradually. ***In a typical turn you will gradually increase the pressure you are exerting on the ski. As you approach the end of the turn you should be exerting the most pressure!***

Practice and memorize the CPCPU technique, and then get out on the groomed runs and experiment with applying different amounts of pressure to your skis, at different speeds. Varying the pressure you put on your skis during the turn is a subtle skill experts use when skiing more difficult terrain. We will talk more about this in later chapters.

Let's review what we have so far:
- ✓ To start the basic carved turn, flex your ankles and move your knees forward **Compressing** the imaginary springs and putting pressure on your skis (**Compress = C**, in C**PCPU**).
- ✓ As part of the compression phase, in fact precisely "*instantly*" after you begin to compress, you will **Point** your knees in the direction you would like to turn (**Point = P**, in C**P**CPU).
- ✓ Now be patient as you **Continuously Push** on the springs to apply pressure on your skis through the whole turn. Also keep pointing the knees until the end of the turn (Continuously Push = **CP**, in CP**CP**U).

We have now arrived at the end of the turn and what happens next is truly refreshing. Because you have pressured your skis through the whole turn, you now have a lot of stored energy built up in them. Use this energy to explode upward out of the turn. This releases the pressure off the front of your boots, which repositions you standing up centered over your skis. This allows your major leg muscles to relax. The duration of this relaxed phase is dependent on the radius and length of your turn, the steepness of the hill, and what you are trying to ski around (as in bumps, ruts, or piles of snow) or through (as in crud or powder). It may be a few seconds to only a fraction of a second. This quick relaxation of your leg muscles between turns allows you to use less energy to ski, resulting in less fatigue. Contrast this with the static position must intermediates remain in all the time (no up and down movement) and you can understand why they experience fatigue after only a short distance on challenging terrain. A continuously flexed muscle tires quickly. Remember to relax between turns. Now let's review again.

✓ You are pushing into the end of the turn, with the springs compressed and your knees pointing to the inside of the turn.
✓ To finish the turn stop pushing on the imaginary springs and rebound up off them, back to an upright position over your skis (**Up = U**, in CPCPU).
✓ Your skis are now running flat, not on edge. Relax your leg muscles for an instant.
✓ Initiate the new turn by compressing the imaginary springs toward your ski tips. This starts the next CPCPU carved turn sequence.
✓ Point your knees in the direction of the new turn.
✓ Push through to the end of the new turn.
✓ Explode (rebound) off the imaginary springs, finishing the turn.

TIP: Remember to vary the amount of pressure or pushing you exert on your skis to control the turn. Be sure to gradually increase the pushing force on your skis until the end of the turn. The most force comes at the end of the turn. Experiment with it on groomed snow to attain enlightenment (so to speak.)

By now some ski professionals reading this are probably about to doubt my ability to teach you to turn, because I have not mentioned weighting and un-weighting of the skis to aid the tipping phase as you get your skis on the edge. I have waited for just the right time to talk to you about this part of carving turns.

If you repeatedly practice the CPCPU drill, discussed on the previous two pages, you will be weighting and un-weighting your skis naturally, without having to think about it and the carved turns will just happen. However, if we can create an in-depth understanding, for you, of how you transfer weight from ski-to-ski, you will be able to more effectively edge your skis. Effective edging enables you to become outside ski dominant, substantially increasing your control.

So, at this point, there are two things I want you to be aware of when it comes to weighting and un-weighting. First, during the CPCPU sequence, the weighting of the ski occurs during the Continuous Pressure phase of the turn and the un-weighting happens during the Up phase when you return to a nearly upright position, standing centered on a flat ski. Secondly, the weighting/un-weighting process usually has more to do with **WEIGHT SHIFTING,** in which you are always transferring the weight from the ski doing most of the carving to the ski initiating the next turn.

Relaxation is a big part of carving turns, so it is very important to always utilize your upper body engrams (the correct body positions learned in Part One) to achieve the correct stance over your skis. With that said, I am going to limit this discussion to just two types of weight shifting: The Skate and Shift, and what I like to call the Subtle Shift to Flat Foot.

The Skate and Shift

Imagine yourself ice skating down the frozen canal like Hans Brinker. Most of us can picture Hans as he pushes his skates from side to side, moving quickly across the ice. Each stride is propelled by his leg, and then it stretches to hold the glide for as long as possible. Meanwhile his free skate is pulled gracefully through the air to take up residence next to his gliding skate. Then he thrusts this free leg out to the side, contacts the ice, and standing on this leg he begins the glide again. This same motion is used to skate on skis, as illustrated in Figure 8.2 below.

You can practice skating as you make your way around the mountain.

Figure 8.2 *Skate and shift to carve. This illustration shows one complete skating sequence on skis, but it looks suspiciously like a carved turn of sorts. With practice you will be able to reduce the size of the skate, turning it in to a small step after which you simply hang on for the ride through a carved turn.*

The skate and shift is a simple way to un-weight one ski and transfer the weight to the other ski. This really is an easy maneuver to learn, as it is just a series of linked glides from ski to ski, while keeping your skis angled out in a V.

Now get ready to turn skating into carving. This is going to happen almost completely without you thinking about it. As you step out onto the gliding ski, you will need to do one additional movement. Combine your stepping out, with standing up. In the above illustration you can see the skier comes from legs compressed or bent to an upright position as he/she transfers their weight to the new gliding ski. Think of it as stepping out toward the other side of the V, and at the same time stand tall onto the newly weighted ski. Now, get ready to carve.

Converting Skating to a Carved Turn

The big secret to transforming skating into carving is to pull the unweighted boot and ski over close to your gliding (or weighted ski) and **hold** your position. Now, as you learned in Part Two, apply compression to the springs as you weight both skis and point your knees toward the next skate. But, don't take another skating step and just ride your skis through the turn being created by this action.

To summarize, step out onto the glide ski, stand up onto it, and place the unweighted ski next to the glide ski. At this point stand with weight on both skis, but be sure the glide ski is weighted most. Push your knees forward (compressing the springs) as you point (or rotate) your knees into the turn. The turn will always be toward the inside ski; the one that you lifted over next to the glide ski. REMEMBER THIS IS ONE FLUID AND CONTINUOUS MOTION. SKATE, STEP OVER, COMPRESS, POINT, AND CARVE!

Don't forget to practice the "skate into a carve" in both directions.

Skating is one of a bag of tricks you should practice repeatedly until it becomes second nature to you. Skating is also useful for gaining momentum when the slope becomes too flat, or you need to ski uphill a bit to get to the trail or lift. Other useful ski techniques for getting around the hill are the herringbone, side step, side slip, and kick turn.

The Subtle Shift to Flat Foot (SSFF)

This subtle turning technique is used by expert skiers to make effortless turns in all conditions without any apparent weight transfer from ski to ski. The other thing you will notice about expert skiers using this turn technique is their uncanny ability to make beautiful turns in both directions.

The dynamics of an effortless turn reside in your ability to do a few things simultaneously. Fortunately this is much easier to practice than it may be to explain. To help you get this concept of shifting to a flat foot, I want you to imagine you are just finishing a right turn on skis. The weight is on your left ski as you begin to stand up and transition out of the right turn. At this point, take the weight off your left ski and transition it to the right ski as you apply muscle force with your right leg. At this same instant, push your right foot flat in your ski boot and point your knees in the direction of the new turn. You know you are doing this correctly when you feel pressure under the arch of your foot each time you flatten it. I realize this paragraph may be difficult to understand, so instead of re-reading it I suggest you keep reading and this next paragraph will clarify the concept.

Learning this subtle weight shift and flattening of the foot can be done right in your living room. Begin by finding a pair of running shoes, Birkenstocks, or other shoes with a significant arch pad in the insole. Street shoes probably will not work for this exercise. Before we proceed, I want to warn you to be careful when doing this exercise, because the potential does exist to put excessive pressure on your knees. With your feet unable to glide or move it can create more pressure than doing this exercise on skis, especially if you were to stumble or fall during the exercise. Do not attempt this exercise if you have any medical problems with your knees. With that said, let's learn this subtle shift to a flat foot.

Grab your ski poles and head for the living room. To position yourself, stand with your feet about 5 inches apart and your ankles flexed forward to create a slight bend at the knee. Use your ski poles for support by placing them wide and out in front of your feet by about ten inches. Place all your weight on your left foot as you slowly push your knees a bit more forward and point them to the right. Hold this position and press your left foot flat until you feel the pressure under your arch. Remember to keep all of your weight on your left foot throughout this part of the exercise using your right foot only to maintain balance. Next you are going to shift your weight to your right foot. To do this straighten your legs, *lift your left heel slightly* (very important) and step down on your right foot as you bend your knees forward again, pointing them to the left. Hold this position with all your weight now on your right foot while you press your right foot flat. Do you feel the pressure under your right arch? When performing this exercise correctly it will develop enough pressure under the arch of the foot to create minor discomfort.

On the other hand, if you are having trouble feeling pressure under the arch of your weighted foot, you may want to try taping a 1" x 1" piece of foam about a 1/4" thick under the arch pad of your shoe insole. This will help you feel the pressure under your arch when you weight and flatten your foot.

If you still can't feel significant pressure under your arch, most likely one of two things is wrong. First, you may not be pointing your knees far enough in the direction of the un-weighted foot. This is important in that if you can not create pressure under your arch in this exercise, then you also will not be creating enough pressure on the inside edge of your ski as you attempt to carve turns on the snow. As you point your knees to one side or the other during this exercise, discontinue it immediately if you feel even slight discomfort.

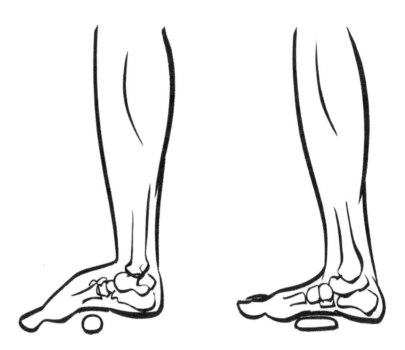

Figure 8.3 *Shift Weight and Flatten Foot. The foot on the right has been flattened out to facilitate transferring pressure to the edge of the weighted ski. This is accomplished by transferring your weight onto one foot and then pointing your knees in the direction of the un-weighted foot. The ball is compressed by the foot that has been flattened.*

If pointing your knees more failed to increase pressure under your arch, your problem may be caused by the shape of your foot. If it varies much from the norm you simply may not be able to develop the desired pressure under your arch without the aid of custom footbeds. To remedy this situation you need to see a foot professional about getting custom footbeds (for more on this see chapter 23 titled Correct Alignment is First). ***Don't forget to take the foam out of your shoes after doing this exercise.***

For a moment imagine you are back on the slopes and ready to practice the SSFF (Subtle Shift to Flat foot). As you complete a ski turn, stand up on both skis and slightly lift the heel of your previously weighted downhill ski, while transferring your weight to the other ski. Immediately flatten your weighted foot to help develop pressure on the inside edge of your newly weighted ski. Feel the pressure under your arch. Now, and I mean right now, apply CPCPU! Remember, C = Compress by driving your knees forward, P = Point you knees in the direction you want to turn, CP = apply Continuous Pressure through to the end of the turn, and U = stand Up riding equally weighted flat skis, positioned to begin the next turn. Congratulations! You just added the Subtle Shift and Flat Foot to CPCPU.

Think of creating carved turns as a very fluid and continuous motion. As you practice the SSFF weight shift exercise at home, concentrate on making it a rhythmic and continuous movement from the left foot to the right foot. Repetition is a good thing, so practice this *secret to creating a carved turn (SSFF)* many times, and then practice some more. It is helpful to measure your progress in writing. To do this we suggest you decide on the number of times you will practice this drill at home. After you have decided on a number, write it down, and keep a log until you have reached the desired number of practice sequences.

We suggest doing between 50 and 100 repetitions of this dry land practice sequence before you take it to the snow. It takes time to create the mental and physical side of the engram for this movement, so we also suggest you do this in sets of 10 or 15. There are several advantages to chunking it out in smaller sets. It gives you time to absorb it into your mind between sets, and it helps you avoid straining any body parts by doing too many repetitions in one session. Doing one of these dry land training sets per day is appropriate. Be sure to do it in slow motion so you will not leave out any steps.

This is the most important dry land training you will do in this book. It is going to create the mental memory portion of your "basic carved turn" engram. If you feel you are unable to do this exercise physically, it can still be memorized using the bed time visualization method described on page 22.

Developing the CPCPU turn using the Subtle Shift to Flat Foot weight transfer technique will prepare you for learning the advanced RAT turn techniques discussed later in this book. The RAT (Relaxed Aggressive Turn) contains the final three elements needed to complete your advanced turn repertoire.

Be aware that this dry land practice drill is isometric in nature requiring that you flex and hold some muscles in specific positions for up to twenty to thirty seconds per sequence. If this begins to fatigue you, reduce your number of repetitions per set, as necessary, to allow you to do it correctly without losing focus due to muscle strain. If you feel any discomfort in your knees, reduce the force you are exerting during the Pointing phase. If discomfort lasts for any length of time discontinue this dry land exercise.

DRY LAND PRACTICE DRILL: CPCPU with Subtle Shift to Flat Foot

1. Stand with your feet 5 – 7 inches apart and place your ski poles ten inches in front of you. Make sure the poles are also about 8 inches wider than your body on each side.
2. While supporting yourself with your ski poles, bend your knees comfortably forward.
3. Lift your left heel slightly, and apply most of your weight to the right foot.
4. Push your right foot flat as you point your knees to the left.
5. Continue to apply forward pressure to the inside arch of your right foot.
6. Use your leg muscles to keep your knees driving forward and to the left, and to exert pressure on the arch of the right foot for at least 3 seconds
7. Next stand Up straight and apply equal weight to both legs.
8. Start the sequence again by bending you knees comfortably forward.
9. Now lift your right heel slightly, and apply most of your weight to the left foot.
10. Push your left foot flat as you point your knees to the right.
11. Continue to apply forward pressure to the inside arch of your left foot.
12. Use your left leg to keep your knees driving forward and to the right for 3 seconds. Then, stand up straight.
13. This completes two turns, one to the left, followed by one to the right.
14. Finally, create a log and track your progress as discussed on page 60.

DISCONTINUE THIS EXERCISE IF YOU FEEL ANY DISCOMFORT.

As we move through the next few chapters you will add edging, the left-right hip slide, and aggressive relaxation, giving you all the tools necessary to carve advanced turns. On our way to discovering the RAT turn we do need to spend some time on Edging and Body Mass Utilization. So, if you're ready, let's jump on our edges.

CHAPTER 9

EDGING: Lean Em Over Then Do the Up Down Around

Let's all take a moment and profusely thank ski manufacturers for continually pouring money into the R & D well. The net result of an endless pursuit for the perfect ski has been the development of the Shape Ski. However, technological advances in ski design carry with it the proverbial double edged sword. On one side we have the benefit of a ski that is much easier to get on edge, yet because of this benefit, many of you are lazy edgers. Lazy edging works just fine on groomed beginner and intermediate runs. But when the skiing gets challenging, things go downhill much faster than a lazy edger can control.

What do we do? Well, I suggest you go back to your living room and bring your skis, boots, bindings, and poles with you. Before we start, let me remind you to keep your hands spread wide while leaning on your poles for balance. Make sure there isn't any furniture near by to hit your head on if you fall. This exercise is pretty safe, but I am always paranoid about possible mishaps, so humor me and be careful.

Lay your skis on a flat floor and, with your boots on, step into your bindings. Begin by bending your knees forward and apply pressure to the front of your boots. Not much happens. Although your skis flex a bit, they don't really move anywhere because it is too difficult to overcome all the resistance created by your boots, bindings, and skis. Next, lean back slightly and apply pressure to the back of your boots, and again not much happens to the ski.

So far so boring, but the action starts now. With your poles firmly planted out to each side of your body for support, lean over to one side. Your ski edges should immediately come off the floor. Wha-la! Edging is really that simple. Lean to the right and the skis' left edges come off the floor; lean to the left and the skis' right edges come off the floor. The point here is edging can be accomplished by simply tilting or leaning to one side or the other. Yet, to create good carved turns on a variety of terrain **it takes more than just tipping the skis on edge.**

Leaning, tipping or tilting your skis on edge is fine on easy runs and any of these methods will create enough edge pressure to make a basic turn. What these edging methods will not allow you to do is create a good carved turn in challenging terrain. To improve your edging technique you need to add some hip action to the CPCPU turning method. This can be accomplished by simply sliding your hips to the inside of the turn immediately after you compress forward and point your knees in the turn direction. Well, I didn't mean to get into the hips just yet, but it is never too early to start thinking hips, and we will get into the details soon.

One reason we had you practice the CPCPU in the previous chapter was to help you learn the basic movements needed to put you in a position over your skis that will allow you to edge correctly throughout the entire turn.

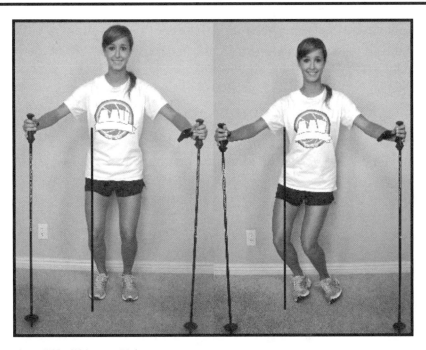

Figure 9.1 *Tilt Skis on Edge. The feet pictured on the left are flat. The feet pictured on the right are on edge. Notice that the model's hips have also shifted to her right helping her knees get the skis up on edge. This hip shift is shown by the lines drawn on the photo. In an advanced turn the knees only assist in this process, while the hips create much of the force to edge the skis.*

Remember the **CP** part of the turn? **C**ontinually **P**ushing through the turn not only helps you stay in control, but it transfers a lot of the work to the ski. After you initiate the turn, combined with sliding your hips to the inside of the turn, you then add more power through the continuous push phase and your skis will bite or edge into the snow with more force, which in skiing translates to more control. In figure 9.1 the model on the right has combined the **C** (Compress), and the **P** (Point), causing her hips to slide passed her shoe edges. If she were on skis and using the CPCPU technique, her hips would be passively sliding to the inside of the turn every time. Later, in Chapter Ten, you will learn how to make this passive hip slide an active part of your carved turn, so don't worry about understanding the hip slide technique at this point as we continue our discussion about edging.

I think we can all agree that getting your skis on edge is not a big deal, and the same can be said for getting off your edges. But, it does become a big deal when you don't get off (or release) your edges at the end of every turn. You may have guessed by now that we put the U in CPCPU just to teach you to release your edges between turns. At the end of every turn comes the "UP" or un-weighted transition between turns. During this transition your skis must be flat and completely off their edges. Releasing the ski edges enables expert skiers to smoothly move from turn to turn.

Figure 9.2 *Spring Up and Down.* *This up and down motion helps you get on and off your edges. Remember to apply the CPCPU technique to create the entire turn.. From the top of the illustration, the skier is in the turn and then stands up tall to transition to the next turn where he again compresses the springs and points his knees in the direction of the new turn.*

Contrast this with skiers that do not effectively release their edges between turns and you will see that they must compensate by stepping,

64

wedging, or even jumping from one ski to the other. To help release your edges between turns, think about your body being on a rollercoaster, albeit a small one, as you go from turn to turn. A roller coaster goes up and down along the track. More specifically, roller coasters usually go up a hill and then down the other side and around a corner at the bottom of the hill. So, I guess we are saying the coaster car goes up, down, and around. That is also exactly what you need to do as you proceed from one turn to the next. The good news here is you already know how to do this, because you have previously learned how to use the CPCPU technique to create turns. At the end of your turn you just need to remember to stand up and ride on two flat skis (no edging). A great advantage to learning this flat ski transition is it allows you to keep your skis on the snow while going from turn to turn. In challenging terrain you will do much better if you don't need to lift one ski each time you want to start a new turn. The alternative to lifting a ski is to use CPCPU turn dynamic.

Think about compressing down into the turn and standing up out of the turn. Yep, this is the down and up of it all. Or, if you prefer, call it up and down. The key point to remember here is that all the action is happening from your hips down. Your knees and legs are creating all the up and down motion while your upper body remains quiet. Your legs are just two large springs that compress when you turn and always want to come back to an upright position when the turn finishes. If you think about it you realize there is a lot of force pushing back on your legs from under the skis during a turn.

To better understand the concept of stored energy use, stand about eighteen inches from the wall and place both hands on it at about chest level or a little higher. Carefully lean into the wall while supported by your arms, and hold that position for a few seconds. You are storing energy in your hands and arms that you will use to push away from the wall when you are ready. If this energy was not available you could not push away and stand up straight again.

Likewise, to make carved turns you need to release the stored energy under your skis. Just like pressing against the wall you press against your skis building and then storing energy through the entire arc. Then, to transition from one turn to the next you release this energy by relaxing your leg muscles which causes your legs to rebound back to their natural upright position. At this point you are standing tall over a flat ski and are ready to initiate another turn. But wait, there's more.

We still need to talk about the around. The first step is to define the *around*. For the purpose of this discussion we will define *around* as the replacement word for the phase "carving a round turn." *Around* is that seldom understood part of the turn that actually occurs simultaneously with the down phase, followed by you standing up at the end of the turn. I am guessing you have heard it uttered from many an aspiring ski instructor to simply go "up and around" on your skis. I always wondered what happened to the down. What we really have here is the Up, Down, and Around. After standing up at the end of a turn you compress down and point your knees in the direction of the new turn to create the carve (or Around). As you remember, to create the "around" you continuously push on your skis to arc through the entire turn. It is during this pushing phase that you will also apply pressure to the inside edge of your downhill ski, using what you learned from the Subtle Shift to Flat Foot Drill on page 61. You will recall how this drill taught you to apply force under your arch by flattening your foot on the weighted (or downhill) ski in the turn. But wait, are the hips doing anything? Yes they are, and for now suffice it to say the hips move sideways helping drive your edges around the turn. Again we are talking about the hips sliding laterally to the inside of the turn. We will explore this more completely in our discussion about body mass movement, but for now take a look at Figure 9.3.

Figure 9.3 *Tip Your Skis on Edge.* *The skier's hips have moved to the inside of the turn creating tremendous edge angulation.*

Your ability to continually put pressure on your edges creates the around or arc of the turn. Begin applying pressure to your edges as soon as you shift weight onto the downhill ski by using the flat foot technique. These actions force the ski's sidecut to engage the snow, allowing it to create an arc until you choose to release the ski edge or you have ridden the turn so long you are now going back uphill and come to a stop.

Figure 9.4 Subtle Shift to Flat Foot. In transition between turns, with the skis running flat, the upper skier lifts his left ski tail off the snow to initiate the weight shift. In the lower illustration the skier has now transferred his weight to the downhill ski while flattening his foot on this ski to enhance edging, as he begins to compress and point the knees into the next turn.

At Mount Hood in August, Mark Kraley demonstrates the proper body position during a pole plant traverse drill. As Mark traverses across the hill he plants only the downhill pole. You can use this exercise to get your skis on edge by moving your hips uphill. See the drill on pages 68 and 69.

To develop your edging skills you can practice the following two on-snow drills that will give you tools to put your skis on edge.

CONTINUOUS PLANT TRAVERSE: Edge Feel Development

1. To begin find a moderately steep groomed slope.
   (be sure you can see other skiers far up the hill when you are traversing)
2. Stand facing across the hill and weight your downhill ski.
3. Before you start, apply pressure to the inside edge of the downhill ski.
   (Use the subtle shift to flat foot to apply pressure, with about 80% of
    your weight on the downhill ski.)
4. Push off traversing across the hill at a very minor downhill angle.
5. Keep your uphill ski slightly ahead of and parallel to the downhill ski.
6. **CREATING THE EPIPHANY!**
   a. Reach out with the downhill pole, as illustrated in the photo on
       page 67. Begin making repeated pole plants, on the downhill
       side only, as you traverse.
   b. Lower your downhill shoulder reaching with your hand to touch
       the pole to the snow. As you get comfortable with this move begin
       to reach farther downhill to plant your pole.
   c. Notice that your hips move toward the uphill in order to stay
       over your skis, allowing your body to stay balanced as you do this
       exercise across the hill (the epiphany).
   d. At this point you should feel your skis edge more strongly. If not,
       study the photo on page 67 and then repeat the exercise until you
       feel the edge pressure increase during the continuous downhill pole plant.
   e. Keep practicing this traverse, with the repeated downhill pole plant
       and your will soon feel the increased force on the inside edge of your
       downhill ski. Remember that this increase in force was created
       mainly by your hips moving or sliding toward the uphill direction to
       keep you in balance during this exercise.
7. Practice it in both directions across the hill.

**PRACTICE THIS REPEATEDLY IN A VARIETY OF SNOW
CONDITIONS AND YOU WILL BE THANKFUL WHEN YOU
ARRIVE AT THE "ADVANCED TURN" SECTION OF THIS BOOK.**

Figure 9.5 *Body Position for Continuous Pole Plant. Skier is traversing across the hill during this exercise. She reaches downhill to plant her pole, causing her hips to move uphill. This increases the angle of her uphill edges.*

By now it is no surprise that if I give you two drills in a row it is very important to learn the first drill before attempting the second one. It is especially true with this next exercise because it takes a complete understanding of *The Continuous Pole Plant Drill* before you can learn the second edging lesson. Ok, I will stop preaching and get down to business. In this exercise you are going to find yourself on the serious end of the turning experience. The good news is this drill will help make it easier for you to really start to feel what it takes to understand advanced turn dynamics. To successfully do this drill you will need to transfer 100 percent of your weight to your downhill or *stance* ski. A ski with all your body weight on it will allow you to more readily feel the ski's edge bite into the snow, helping you to develop a better feel for a complete carved turn. Of course this is only a given if you continue to weight the ski through the entire turn **and stay balanced over the outside ski.** The following drill will give you the tools to do both!

POWER TURNING ON ONE FOOT

1. To begin, find your favorite long, wide groomed run.
2. Now it is time to apply everything you have learned so far.
    a. Start by skiing leisurely down the run, and after a few turns begin to carve nice long round turns with a little more weight on your downhill leg.
    b. Next, transfer 70% of your weight to the outside ski. This feels like you have more weight on your downhill ski, but you can still feel some weight on your uphill ski.
    c. On the next run really start to push on that downhill ski through every turn. Put some aggression into it.
    d. Now make a run skiing with 100 percent of your weight on the downhill or stance ski using the following technique.
3. The Trick: Use the skill you learned in the previous traverse drill to lean out over the downhill ski while moving your hips uphill to stay in balance.
4. Using "The Trick" will enable you to link turns with 100 percent of your weight on the downhill or stance ski, and still stay in balance.
5. Figure 9.6 on page 71 shows the correct body position for this exercise.

Any problems with the previous drill? If so, there are two things you can do. First I would suggest you review the Subtle Shift to Flat Foot and the Continuous Plant Traverse drills. Practice both until the movements become automatic. These are the drills that teach you to effectively transfer weight from ski to ski, and feel the edge of your weighted ski. If this does not produce results, then I would suggest you immediately read the section on alignment in the Equipment Chain section of this book (page 182). Your inability to perform this drill may stem from a body alignment problem. Don't worry; most minor alignment problems can be corrected by a specialist. Your local specialty ski shop may have people on staff that can help you, or they will be able to recommend someone.

Figure 9.6 *A Power Turn on One foot.* *The hips move laterally to the inside of the turn (uphill), as the upper body moves toward the downhill ski to keep the skier in balance over the weighted ski. This turn requires a skier to move at a moderate speed or above to create enough momentum to stay in balance.*

Chapter 10

CROSSING OVER: Body Mass Utilization

Moving your own body mass back and forth across your skis is a major breakthrough in the game of carving turns. But alas, the great majority is afraid of this movement on skis and never achieves it because they are reluctant to become human metronomes. If you ever took piano lessons as a child you know what I am referring to when I say metronome. It is the mechanical device that makes repeated clicking sounds as its single arm swings back and forth marking rhythm for you. Think of this single arm as you and the base it is attached to as your skis. As this arm (or in this case you) swings back and forth across your skis, you are actually moving your body mass from turn to turn.

Figure 10.1 *Think of Yourself as a Human Metronome: The skier above swings back and forth across their skis like the metronome arm swings back and forth across its base. The skier transfers body mass from side to side using lateral hip movements to help edge the skis.*

When ski instructors talk about moving your body mass they are referring to the movement of the center or core of your body. This center is composed of your hips, buttocks, and abdomen. The movement of your body mass from side to side is often referred to as the *crossover maneuver*. This area of your body is very efficient at supplying the movements needed to create quality turns.

To visualize your body core in action, imagine your hips trapped in a long box that is only about as thick as you are front to back at your hips, but extends out from each of your sides by three feet. In other words your hips are now trapped in a big rectangular box. Next imagine your hips can only move from side to side in the box, or to put it another way the hips can only slide laterally back and forth inside this box. Figure 10.2 will help you visualize this sliding action.

Figure 10.2 *Hip Slides in a Box. Sliding the hips from side to side shifts your body mass across your skis from the inside of one turn to the inside of the next turn. This is also referred to as the crossover move. There is some up and down movement of the hips because the legs are elongating at the end of a turn and bending or compressing into and through the turn.*

Now think back to the illustration in figure 8.1 on page 51. This illustration showed you how to create a carved turn using the CPCPU method. You will also remember that you were asked to keep pressure on the imaginary springs throughout the entire turn. This is called the Continuous Push phase of CPCPU. The reason you need to keep pushing through the turn is your skis are pushing back with force, necessitating you keep pressure on them. If not, your ski will want to skid the last half of the turn and you will lose some control over the terrain.

Disco Nights Move

To really drive home this point about the hips moving from side to side, as you turn, I want you to try a neat on-snow drill that will quickly let you feel the correct hip position in the turn. I call this drill the "Disco Nights Move." It gets its name from the famous dance sequence in the movie *Saturday Night Fever*. During a dance scene, the star of the film has his hips swinging back and forth as he points to the sky with one arm and carries his other arm near or on his hip. I hope you know what I am talking about here because you will be using a move very similar to this on the snow to develop a feel for hip placement during the turn. The only difference being you will be pointing your arm more straight out, rather than up toward the sky.

For this drill, put your poles aside and find a gentle, groomed run. Begin by making a series of medium size turns placing your hand on the hip over your downhill or outside ski during every turn. While this is happening take your other arm and point it toward the inside of the turn at about the height of your shoulder. Switch arms every time you start a new turn. It's like this; when you are turning to the right your left hand is on your left hip, and when you are turning to the left your right hand is on your right hip. This switching of the arms automatically makes your hips slide from side to side. Excellent!

As a warm-up to the on-snow drill try this move right in your living room and you will immediately feel your hips move side to side as you switch arms. **Your hips always slide in the direction you are pointing.** To ensure your hips move laterally, point your arm at a slight upward angle and with some enthusiasm. Bend your knees a bit, and let your body adjust so your feet don't move as you switch hands on the hips and point to the other side with your arm.

Disco Nights Move On-Snow Drill

1. Pick a gentle groomed slope, and put your poles aside.
2. To begin, traverse across the hill with your downhill hand on your hip and your uphill arm pointing up the hill.
3. Do this several times while traversing in both directions.
4. Now ski down the gentle slope making turns using this arm and hand position. Be sure to change hand positions between each turn, and always point to the inside of the turn.
5. In between each turn stand up as you reverse the position of your arms.
6. Compress into the next turn keeping your hand on your hip, and your opposite arm pointing to the inside of the turn.

TIP: Be sure to switch the **hand on hip-arm point** position during the UP phase of the turn. See figure 10.3. Did I make that point three times? Oh well, repetition is good.

Racers practice this drill, so don't feel silly as you do it. I did promise in the beginning of this book I would not make you look silly doing on-snow exercises, but this is the one exception because you will benefit tremendously from this exercise.

Figure 10.3 *Disco Nights Move: During each turn the skier points to the inside of the turn, while keeping the outside hand on the hip. Stand tall on your skis and switch hands between every turn.*

You will remember we talked about every turn creating force that tries to push your legs back to the straight up or natural position. The amount of force that is generated is directly related to your speed and the pitch of the slope. The idea here is to be aware that this force is always present and pushing back at you in the turns. This is great because you can use this force to stand up at the end of the turn and slide your hips laterally from the inside of your current downhill ski to the inside of your new downhill ski to initiate the next turn. Say what? Sentences like that last one are a bit disconcerting in that they always make turning on skis sound so difficult. Think of body mass movement like this:

1. Edge aggressively through the turn.
2. At the end of the turn, stand up and slide your hips in the direction of the next turn.
3. If you are finishing a right turn, slide your hips to the left.
4. Coming out of a left turn, slide your hips to the right.
5. You guessed it: Your hips are sliding in the direction of the turn.

Wow! Correct me if I am wrong, but I think the previous four steps give us a great way to do the Up, Down, and Around that we talked about previously. You press down into the turn, pressure your edge around (through) the turn, and then come up onto flat skis as you slide your hips across your skis to help initiate the next turn. I think it's time for a couple of drills that will develop the proper engrams. Let's start with an off-snow drill you can do right in the hallway of your home. During this drill you will be sliding your hips left and right without moving your feet. However, your feet will rotate up on edge with each slide. If this movement creates any uncomfortable sensations, discontinue it. You may feel some light pressure above the outside edge of your hips at the end of each slide due to the angle this drill creates between your upper and lower body. This is the angle referred to when talking about hip angulation. That last statement brings us dangerously close to an opportunity to talk about hips and angles, but I am not going to bite and start talking technical. We will address this in Part Three because of the advanced nature of the material in that section.

HIP SLIDE AWARENESS OFF-SNOW DRILL

1. To begin stand in your hallway equal distance from each side wall.
2. Reach out and put your hands flat on each wall for support.
3. Place feet about 5 or 6 inches apart and flex your ankles forward in order to bend your knees slightly, keeping your hips centered over your feet..
4. Gently slide your hips side to side.
5. As you finish each slide your feet will want to come up on their edges.
6. Go ahead and allow your feet to tilt on edge.
7. At the completion of a slide, stop and hold your position.
8. Look down and you will see that the edge of your hip closest to the wall is roughly 4 to 8 inches past the outside edge of your foot.
9. Do 5 sets of 15 slides over a 2-3 day period.

AT THE END OF EACH SLIDE YOUR CORE BODY MASS IS NOT OVER YOUR FEET. IT IS EITHER 4-8 INCHES LEFT OR RIGHT OF YOUR FEET.

The hip slide awareness you have created by doing the hall way drill can now by used to practice the same lateral hip slide move on the snow. It is really just dancing. It's the "hip-slide" dance.

HIP SLIDE AWARENESS ON-SNOW DRILL

1. To set the stage, start with a series of hockey stops in alternating directions. (In other words do a stop facing the right side of the run, and then do it facing the left side.)
2. Next, do one hockey stop after another as a continuous movement, turning the stops into a series of jerky turns. Be sure to stand up and face the fall line between turns.
3. Do several series with increasing intensity, trying to make a spray of snow. (Notice your body mass moves farther to the inside of the turn as the "Stop Intensity" increases.)
4. Up the intensity of the stops until the spray of snow gets large, or if on firm snow until the skis jerk and chatter a bit under the force of the hockey stops.
5. Be careful not to exert so much force that it becomes uncomfortable or painful.

After doing the hockey stop drill, you should be comfortable with the feeling of your body mass moving farther to the inside of the turn. In fact, I personally have slammed on the brakes so hard using the hockey stop that my uphill hand actually touched the snow, meaning my body mass was deep in the hole. **The hole is the imaginary pit that encompasses all the space inside the arc of your turn.** During this aggressive hockey stop my body mass was pushed toward the inside of the turn (into the hole) with such great force that I had to extend my hand to keep from actually falling over.

This notion of the "hole" is a good way to define all the area inside the half circle arc of a carved turn. The hole is where your hips will be going when you start generating high speed super carved turns. I like the hole analogy because your hips are actually falling down into the space inside each turn. The hips move closer and closer to the ground as the force coming from the turn increases. This force increase is in direct correlation to the speed you are moving and the edge pressure you are exerting on the skis.

To keep pressure on your edges and avoid collapsing into the hole, make sure your shoulders are always parallel to the slope you are descending and that you are facing down the fall line.

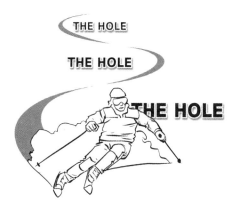

Figure 10.4 *Hips Slide into the Hole. The inside of the turn is often referred to as the hole. The more power the skier generates in the turn, the deeper the hips slide into the hole. The shoulders always remain parallel to the angle of descent.*

CROSSOVER ON-SNOW DRILL: Hip Slide Turns With Hockey Stop Intensity

1. To begin pick a moderate slope that has been groomed.
2. Make one run linking gentle turns using the hip slide technique you learned in your hallway..
3. KEY POINT: The easy way to lean your lower body is to slide the hips.
6. Picture this as you turn; compress your knees and slide the hips to the inside of the turn in one continuous movement!
7. The illustration In Figure 10.2 on page 73 shows the hips sliding side-to-side in the box. The slide happens right after you weight the ski.
9. If you are struggling to perfect this move, you can widen your stance a little to improve your hip slide from side to side (groomed run only).

Be sure to practice the Crossover On-snow Drill on moderate terrain at a slow to medium rate of speed. Doing it faster may feel easier, but you must be careful to remain in control. Even the slightest loss of control during this drill is a sure sign you are skiing too fast.

Most intermediate skiers don't use the crossover or body mass movement to facilitate good turns. Why? Because their approach to skiing is to be one big tense muscle that always remains in a static position. If you are going to master the crossover move you need to remember to approach the crossover technique with some intensity. Utilizing the CPCPU turn will help you generate the power you need to get the crossover going from turn to turn. Leave your old static style behind, and start to do some visible up and down movements as you begin a turn (GO DOWN) and as you complete a turn (COME UP). Relax and stop being a static locked-in-one-position-all-the-time skier. Expert skiing is as smooth and fluid as ballroom dancing, and you have complete license to make up the moves. Everyone develops their own style; loosen up and find yours. We ski with many excellent all mountain skiers, and although they all look great, no two have the same style or identical look to their skiing.

As you develop the fine art of edging and carving, you will begin to ski with less effort. However, developing any skill to its highest level requires practice and a structured approach. Practicing is easy, but it encompasses more than just go skiing as much as you can.

Almost every skier believes that just going skiing frequently is the key to improvement. A much better approach is to add structure to your practice by laying out a plan for improvement before you go to the slopes. From our perspective, the best way to do this is to continually work on the engram development talked about throughout this book. At this juncture in the book we have talked about five body positions and six body movements that require engram development. Just to review here's the list:

Body Positions
1. Hands – Teacup Grip.
2. Arms – Beach ball position.
3. Head – Always floating up like a balloon.
4. Upper Body – Quiet, facing down the fall line/direction of travel.
5. Lower Body – Continually flexing and rebounding

Body Movements
1. Pole Plant – Flick it, stab it, and release it.
2. CPCPU Turn – Creates the Up, Down, and Around of a turn.
3. Skate and Shift – Leads to the basic carved turn.
4. Subtle Shift to Flat Foot – Develops weighting and un-weighting of skis.
5. Hip Slide – Enhances edging through the hip slide crossover move.
6. Body Mass Movement – Rhythmic back and forth movement from turn to turn.

We are really talking about making these positions and movements an involuntary and automatic part of your skiing. Only specific practice on snow will assure all these engrams are retained in the forefront of your subconscious. Skiing is unique in that many times we go long periods between visits to the ski hill and at least once a year that break can exceed six months. With these long periods between ski experiences our engrams seem to drift deep down into our subconscious. To reawaken them we must use our structured approach at the beginning of each new ski day. The structured approach we use to keep our engrams sharp is:

1. Make warm-up runs on an easy groomed slope.
2. During warm-up runs practice each body position one at a time:
a. Beach Ball arms.
    b. Teacup grip.
    c. Head pulled up as if it is a floating balloon.
    d. Upper body facing down the fall line.
    e. Eyes looking forward.
    f. Slight curve in your lower back, shoulders relaxed.
    g. Stomach in, and upper body erect. Don't slump over.
    h. Flick your pole plants with your wrist.
    i. Keep your upper body still - quiet is good.
    j. Practice CPCPU turning technique. Exaggerate up-down.
    k. Next focus on the hip slide technique.
  3. Finally ski an entire run practicing the crossover, with hip
     slide from side to side.

Ok, so you are finished warming up and the lifts are closing. Just kidding, but when we hang the whole list out there to be seen all at one time, it is overwhelming. It is best to chunk it out and practice a little at a time. Just be absolutely sure you think about and write down what it is you want to practice most next time you are on the hill. The really big secret is great skiers always make at least one long warm up practice run to get in their comfort zone. If you are an intermediate skier, we suggest you start your warm up runs on beginner slopes or easier intermediate slopes.

Believe me this really works, and the proof is in the pudding so to speak. I know one ex-world champion who, to this day, starts with several warm up runs on easy slopes every time he goes skiing. Part of his structured approach to the warm up is to make a variety of turns while exaggerating his up and down movement. This helps him "find" his edges and make sure he is finishing his turns. Think about it, this guy has skied at a very high level most of his life and he still takes warm up runs on intermediate slopes.

Part Two Summary

- An effective pole plant occurs at the end, not the beginning of each turn. Think of a pole plant as a flick, stab, and release sequence. Using the teacup grip flick the tip of the pole forward toward the next plant. The plant should be wide and out by the tip of your ski. Extend your elbow to make contact with the snow. ***Keep your arms in the beach ball position and plant your pole early to begin the next turn.***

- Turn your skis using **CPCPU.** This is a four part continuous movement composed of: bending your ankles to Compress your knees forward, Pointing your knees in the direction of the turn, Continuously Pushing forward through the turn, and standing Up at the end of the turn. ***Keep those imaginary springs compressed to pressure the front of your skis throughout the entire turn.***

- Being able to transfer your weight from ski to ski is an essential skill. I still practice the Subtle Shift to Flat Foot, and found myself doing it in the kitchen while I was waiting for my toast to pop up the other morning. ***Practice the Skate and Shift (on snow) and the Subtle Shift to Flat Foot (off snow) exercises frequently to develop a feeling for shifting your weight from ski to ski.***

- Moving your body up and down is mandatory if you want to be a great skier. Bend your knees and push down into the turn, and as the turn ends, stand up onto flat skis (no edges titled into the snow). ***Good up and down motion helps you get on and off your edges.***

- The continuous pole plant drill teaches you to move your hips uphill to increase edge force on the downhill ski. This move places your upper body out over your downhill ski. Using skills from this drill will be very helpful when you are doing the one foot power turn. ***Powerful edge sets are created by moving your hips uphill (to the inside of the turn).***

- Don't be afraid to crossover! Slide your hips from side to side to facilitate moving your body mass (core) back and forth across your skis. Edge aggressively through the turn, then stand up on flat skis and slide your hips in the direction of the next turn. ***Your hips always slide*** *in the turn direction. **This sliding moves your body mass back and forth across your skis (body mass movement).***

- Go skiing as much as possible, if only for a few hours a day. Never ever forget to make warm up runs on easy groomed slopes. Include the following positions and movements in your warm up routine. *As you warm up review the following body positions using the simple imagery provided in this book: Hands, Arms, Head, Upper and Lower Body. And, the following body movements: Pole Plant, CPCPU turn, Skate and Shift, Subtle Shift to Flat Foot, Hip Slide, and the Crossover.*

Advance Turn Dynamics: All Types of Skiing

Chapter 11

The RAT TURN: A Relaxed/Aggressive Turn for All Terrain

Re-lax (ri laks'), *v.t.* **1.** to make less tense, rigid, or firm; make lax: *to relax the muscles.*
Ag-gres-sive (e gres' iv), *adj.* **2.** making an all-out effort to win or succeed. **3.** vigorously energetic.

Throughout Parts One and Two we talked about relaxation as an important element of good ski technique, but now it's time to do a little more in depth analysis. Advanced skiers use a relaxed, yet aggressive approach to creating carved turns in any type of snow. Before we go any further into this subject I need to clarify the context in which we will be talking about "Aggressive." Do not think of aggressive as an attitude or a way of attacking an entire ski run. When we use the term we are talking about aggressive edging to create a more powerful turn. To learn to be relaxed and aggressive at the same time, you must first develop a clear understanding of the difference between aggressive and tense. As stated above: Aggressive implies vigor, energy, and a desire to succeed. Being tense connotes being rigid or drawn taut, the opposite of relaxed.

Most intermediate skiers exist in a very timid state and are at best just one challenging turn away from becoming tense. Intermediate skiers don't exert enough force on their edges, causing them to remain trapped in the realm of the skidded turn. When challenged, an intermediate will most often tense up, becoming rigid and ineffective, as compared to relaxed and aggressive. A key to getting out of this trap is to consciously relax between turns and then step on the gas (aggressive edge pressure) as you go through the turn. **Do this correctly and you will feel a floating sensation between turns.** When you are creating sufficient edge pressure to ensure you carve through the entire turn, without a hint of skidding, you can back off and experiment with using a less aggressive edge set to add finesse to your turns. Experts look smooth everywhere because they have learned to apply just the right amount of edging for a given situation.

If an aspiring expert attempts to improve their ski technique on challenging terrain by simply tipping their skis on edge; the net result is no improvement. Yet, once this person adds aggression to the formula it produces the force necessary to carve turns in any condition. They just need to relax and get aggressive, but it is much easier said than done.

To begin your journey toward a more advanced carved turn, you must remember the following tips:

- ✓ During the turn transition keep your shins in a neutral position, centered between the front and back of your upper boot cuff.
- ✓ The range of motion for your shin is from neutral to forward against your front cuff, and never against the back of your boot for more than an instant. You can think of this as a rocking motion (as in rocking chair). But, do not allow this movement to pull your upper body back, causing you to be behind your skis and playing catch up.
- ✓ At the start of the turn, flex your ankle forward to put pressure on the front of your skis.
- ✓ Make sure you have a relaxed grip (teacup style) on your poles.
- ✓ Enter into the turn with a relaxed and correct stance.
- ✓ Apply aggressive pressure to your ski edges throughout the turn.
- ✓ Slide hips right and left to create powerful edging.
- ✓ **You will feel a relaxed floating sensation between turns.**
- ✓ **Apply more pressure to the downhill edge during the turn.**

Figure 11.1 *Aggressive Edging with Hip Slide to the Uphill Side. When executing aggressive carves like this one, the feet are further apart even though the legs are still close together. In addition you will notice the hips slide to the uphill side of the turn, lending power to the edging and helping create the hip angulation needed for this type of turn. The arrow shows the hip angulation created by the upper and lower body, with the common point at the hips.*

You should be starting to feel comfortable with the carved turns you are generating using the CPCPU/Subtle Shift to Flat Foot technique (pages 57-61) and the Hip Slide Side-to-Side crossover move (page 73, fig. 10.2). In order to carve your skis throughout the entire turn, you will use these skills in combination with two new tools. We are going to add the *expert carved turn* dynamic and share with you the secrets to varying your turn size for added control. We will dissect these concepts for you in the next chapter and in chapter 13, we will get deep into the subject of varying your turn size.

It is important to completely understand the *relax* in the Relaxed Aggressive Turn. There are two components to this part of our RAT turn. To start, you must learn to relax the foot and leg of the downhill ski *while it is still weighted*, and secondly you need to have a relaxed hip slide transition between turns. It is nearly impossible to see, but every accomplished skier relaxes their leg muscles and their feet between turns. There are many nuances in this maneuver, but in keeping with our core commitment to simplicity we will only talk about what is needed to accomplish this relaxation phase of the turn.

An expert skier does the RAT turn by simply combining muscle relaxation with a lateral hip slide in the direction of the next turn. Turn initiation starts by relaxing your leg and foot muscle of the weighted downhill ski and is completed using the hip slide to move your body core back across your skis to the inside of the next turn. These two actions happen *just as you stand up at the end of your current turn* and this makes the transition between turns much quicker, while taking less effort. The relaxation of the downhill ski at the end of the turn actually helps trigger the next turn, and if you already have your hips traversing across your skis toward the new turn you are successfully doing the RAT! Sounds like a 50's dance – let's all do the RAT.

REMINDER: At this point in the book it probably goes without saying (but just in case); behind this foot/leg relaxation and hip slide combo-move is the ever-present Down, Around, and Up. Remember, your legs are always flexing *down* into the turn, staying flexed *around* the turn, and finally extending *up* out of the turn. Never forget to do the up and down, the up and down, the up and down, the up and down, the up and down, up and down.............

RAT TURN BREATHING DRILL

1. Link 4 -6* medium size turns on a groomed intermediate run.
2. To initiate the Up phase relax the leg muscles of the weighted downhill ski.
3. Stand up and slide your hips in the direction of the next turn.
4. While in the "Up" transition between turns take a deep breath.
5. During the turn phase exhale strongly yet slowly through pursed lips.
6. As you exhale remember to aggressively pressure your edges (figure 11.1, page 85).

TIP: Stay relaxed as you inhale during the turn transitions.

*TAKE A BREAK BETWEEN TURN SETS & DON'T HYPERVENTILATE.

CHAPTER 12

How Experts Carve Turns

With the RAT turn in our tool box, it is time to pursue the long and short of it; or to be more exact, learning to create both long and short turns almost anywhere at any time. If you follow expert skiers around the mountain not much time passes before you notice several things about their style of skiing. They look great, and this is mainly due to the fact they can turn equally well in both directions, and the size of their turns varies frequently.

Varying the size of a well shaped turn is paramount to high performance skiing. It adds confidence to your skiing through an increased level of control. Being able to vary your turn size without hesitation makes it much more fun to ski narrow sections, steep bowls, bumps, rock strewn areas, and whatever else you can think of. Being able to vary the size of your turns, *while always retaining the same shape to your turn,* is your ticket to enjoying the all mountain ski experience. It is important to realize that turn size varies, but you are always making essentially the same shape in your turns. This shape can best be compared to the letter C without the small up and down curls at the beginning and end of the letter. Another way to think of a shape that best illustrates a completed turn is to imagine a perfect half circle.

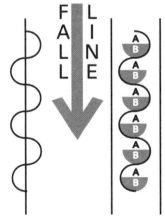

Figure 12.1 *Joined Half Circles*: *The diagram on the left shows a correctly formed side-by-side ski tracks. The diagram on the right shows each turn divided into part A and part B. Part A of the turn is formed above the fall line. Part B, the second half of the turn, is formed below the fall line. In part A you ski into the fall line, while in part B you ski away from the fall line. The fall line is represented by the vertical lines in this illustration. Read on for a complete explanation.*

When skiing directly down the hill, you will be half way through the turn as your skis are pointing down the fall line (part A, fig.12.1). This occurs just before you enter the second half of the turn which then takes you out of the fall line (part B, fig. 12.1). If you look closely at Figure 12.1 you can see that at the end of each turn your skis are facing across the hill. Actually, your skis are in a traverse for just a millisecond between the end of one turn and the beginning of the next turn. The vertical lines in Figure 12.1 represent the fall line.

To clarify the concept of skiing above and below the fall line, you may think of it in another way. In part A, the first half of the turn, you begin skiing slightly across the hill and complete the first half of your turn by carving *into the fall line* with your skis facing downhill for just an instant. This leads into part B of the turn that takes you immediately *out of the fall line*. In part B, you ski away from the fall line as your skis come around into a position facing across the hill. Initiating turns above the fall line allows you to gain control over your skis and carve perfect half circle turns.

> When skiing in the fall line (generally straight down the hill), the first half of the turn ends with your skis pointing downhill. The second half of the turn ends with your skis pointing across the hill. To completely absorb this concept, please study Figure 12.2 carefully.

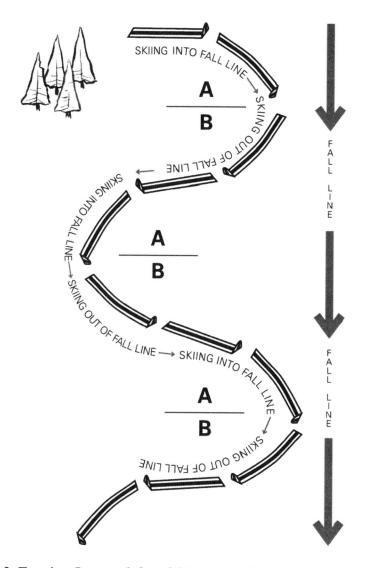

Figure 12.2 *Turning Into and Out Of the Fall Line. Skis are turned down into the fall line in the first half of the turn (A). Skis are turned out of the fall line in the second half of the turn (B). Skis face across the hill at a slight downward angle between turns. The goal is to carve one-half of the turn above the fall line and one-half of the turn below the fall line.*

This concept of making one-half of the turn above the fall line and one-half of the turn below the fall line is very important. Make sure you clearly understand it before you continue into the next section.

Use a Half Turn to Begin a Series of Turns

Expert skiers use a little known or discussed technique to start every run. It is used in all kinds of snow to ensure they can carve perfect turns throughout the run. This secret technique is called a "Check Turn to Begin." Every time experts begin a run, they use a checking half turn to properly set up their entire series of turns. This check turn accomplishes three goals.

First, it is much easier to begin turning from a dead stop if you can ski straight down the hill and need to only complete one half of the turn. As you know, you need momentum or energy to initiate a turn. Unfortunately, when you begin from a dead stop there is no momentum to create the first carved turn, making it much harder to drive the skis through a complete turn. The main reason is you do not have the energy from the **Up** motion (of CPCPU) needed to initiate the first turn.

Second, you can use the checking half turn to load the skis with energy in order to immediately gain control over them, and third, it gives the skier feedback about the condition of the snow. We are talking about conditions such as texture, firmness, and depth (if powder) of the snow. Different types of snow require different amounts of edge force, combined with the correct amount of pressure on the front of your skis. If you are going to ski it like an expert, you need to know how much edge force to use. The *check turn to begin* gives you the necessary feedback needed to determine how you will turn through any type of snow.

Begin a run by first pointing your skis downhill at an angle less than the fall line angle. Call it a soft angle of descent. I suppose you are thinking how can I stand still with my skis pointing almost straight down the hill? Well, you need to be creative. Some ways to do it are as follows:

1. Start on a cat track so your skis are level, yet still facing down the run that is just below you.
2. If you are in the bumps, start by positioning yourself on the side of a bump with the tails of your skis resting in the rut behind you. Again your skis will be almost level and you will not slide forward until you push off.
3. If you are in powder or crud, you can lift one ski up and drive the tail back into the snow until you boot stops it. Repeat this motion with the other ski and you are now facing downhill with the front of your skis sticking out of the snow.

When ready, push forward into the run and immediately make a quick check to complete this first half turn. The check can be compared to a mild hockey stop, which creates the energy for you to stand up and initiate your first complete turn in the fall line. Just remember not to allow your skis to turn completely sideways in this first check turn of the run. Get it?

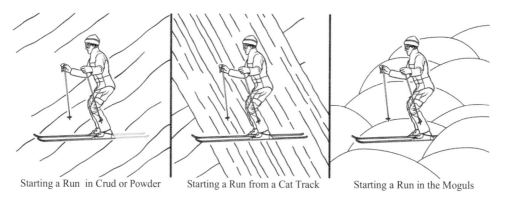

Starting a Run in Crud or Powder Starting a Run from a Cat Track Starting a Run in the Moguls

Figure 12.3 *How to Stand When Starting a Run with a Half Turn Check Maneuver. It always starts with you facing directly down the hill in the fall line.*

A half turn is much easier to initiate at slow speeds, and safely provides you with a lot of information for the rest of the run. For example, if you are starting a powder run it will tell you whether the snow is light or heavy; if you are starting a bump run it will tell you if the snow is soft, firm, or very hard. Then you can use this information to adjust your first full turn to best handle the snow conditions under foot. This is an advanced concept, and takes time to fully understand. But don't despair, as we will revisit the "Half Turn to Begin" in the upcoming sections on Powder, Crud, and Bumps.

LONG TURNS

Long turns develop slower allowing you time to drop your body core further to the inside of the turn. Essentially, you are just using the tools you have acquired so far in this book to make this kind of turn on a groomed run. A long turn is made by applying a slow motion version of the CPCPU turning system in combination with the Subtle Shift to Flat Foot and the Hip Slide Side-to-Side.

In other words, you compress your lower body into the turn and weight your outside ski as you move your body mass to the inside of the long arc you are carving in the snow. While doing all of this, think slow and relaxed, allowing time for the ski to ride through its specific turn radius. For a definition of a ski's turn radius see Chapter 24 titled Boots, Skis and Bindings.

I would suggest you practice riding your skis through a long turn about one thousand times. To accomplish this it will take about two top-to-

92

bottom runs on a large ski mountain. Stay relaxed and enjoy the ride through each and every turn. Making long radius turns on a groomed run is a pretty easy assignment and you probably are already doing this to some extent. During your practice session, feel your skis as you arc through these long turns and notice if your ski is skidding anywhere in the turn. Be patient and let the turn develop.

If you have trouble feeling your skis on edge through the entire turn, enlist the help of friend to watch your skis as you turn, looking for skid marks. Another way to evaluate your turn shape is ski near a chair lift so that you will be able to see your tracks next time you ride up the lift. After locating your tracks, look for a consistently round arc that does not vary in width. If you observe skidding evidence from your track, you need to change the way you pressure your ski edge during the turn. Varying pressure or lack of enough pressure is a sure cause of skidding. To remedy this, focus on increasing the force you exert on your edges during the turn, and make sure this pressure is applied consistently throughout the entire turn. It is easiest to see the tracks you lay down on freshly groomed, un-skied slopes (referred to as untracked corduroy), so get up early and go look at the arcs your skis leave in the snow.

SHORT TURNS

Stomp on, jump on, and attack those ski edges as you quickly steer your feet between turns, like an aggressive slalom racer banging through the gates. Can you feel the energy projected by that last sentence? It is meant to create an image of a forceful and energetic approach to turning your skis, which just happens to be exactly what it takes to make short turns in quick succession.

To make a series of short turns, you need to move your lower body much faster than in larger slower turns. It is time to get aggressive throughout every turn. To do this you will both steer your skis in between turns, and forcefully apply pressure to your downhill ski during the turn. To get your skis to come around more quickly in a short turn you must exert enough pressure on the ski to bend it past its natural sidecut. This enables it to turn in a shorter space.

By increasing the rate and range of your leg extension and flex, you will increase the force generated under your skis during the turn. Feel yourself extend your legs hard out of the turn, and then flex quickly and forcefully down into the new turn. This creates a lot of pressure on the ski and allows it to turn quickly and literally helps push you up out of the turn in short order. I think I have made this point, but just to reiterate; I will say that generating this extra force on your skis bends them into a tighter arc which will send the skis at a greater angle across the fall line during each turn.

Applying aggressive pressure during the turn is only half the battle, for you must also steer your skis while in between turns. This helps you turn more quickly with less energy, because you are helping your skis change direction while you are riding a flat ski. A flat ski is easier to steer because there is no force pushing up at you from your edges as they bite into the snow.

We have waited until now to talk about steering so as not to muddy the water by adding another concept too early in your journey to becoming an expert skier. Instructors may tell you that steering is no longer important because the new shape skis turn so quickly. I will admit steering is less important because of modern skis, but I feel strongly that it is a tool you should still have in your "proverbial" bag. Steering can save you when you are caught in a difficult situation and need a quick escape. For example, when you poorly execute a turn, a quick steer can put you right back on your line down the hill. Steering starts to be very important in the game of expert skiing when you make short radius turns quickly; which by the way is one of the precursors to high performance bump skiing.

The steering of your skis is an easy concept to grasp and apply, as it is simply the application of a twisting motion produced by the feet and legs. The quadriceps and calf muscles create the force used to steer your feet. To feel this sensation stand on a bare floor with your legs together, and without moving your feet, begin to twist your legs to the left and right. Do you feel your quads and calf muscles tightening, and your feet trying to point in the direction of the twist? Exactly!

When you get back on the snow you can help your legs steer by adding some foot steering. This is done by forcing your big toe against the inside of the boot riding on the outside ski as you simultaneously force the little toe of your other foot against the outside edge of the boot riding on the inside ski. See Figure 12.4. Steering the feet uses a different set of muscles and they can be found residing in the front of your lower legs. To feel these muscles at work sit on a bar stool with your legs hanging freely off the edge. Begin to point your feet from side to side, being sure to keep them parallel to the floor, and you will feel the muscles being used in the lower legs during this exercise. To facilitate quick turning remember the following:

- ✓ Keep a quiet upper body and let the lower body do the work.
- ✓ Use a strong up and down leg motion to generate force under the downhill ski. This powerful action will help you rebound up to a flat ski as you transition to the next turn.
- ✓ Steer with the feet and legs when the ski is flat and between turns.

94

- ✓ Use the *Hip Slide in a Box* technique (Figure 10.2, page 73) to help quickly move your body mass from side to side.
- ✓ You must apply CPCPU at rapid fire speed! Compress your legs, Point your knees, Continually Push hard through the short turn, rebound Up and Steer your feet toward the next CPCPU.

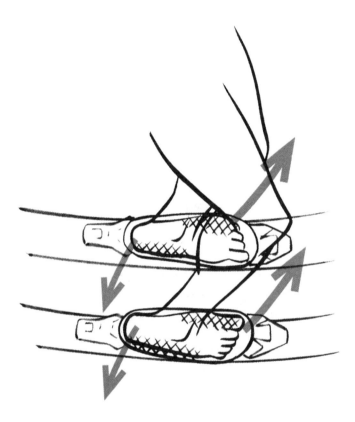

Figure 12.4 *Use Big Toe Little Toe Pressure to Steer Your Skis. The shaded areas on the feet and the arrows show the direction of force applied by the big and little toes to steer a ski through the transition between turns. In this example the skis are being turned to the left.*

When you are executing a series of short turns correctly, you will feel yourself in a constant rhythmic motion with little or no sensation of speeding up, slowing down, or jerkiness. Skiing smoothly and quickly through a set of short turns yields a track in the snow that is symmetrical, with each turn identical to the last. The following line drawing creates a vivid comparison between two wrong ways to shape your turns and the only right way to do it.

Figure 12.5 *Turn Shapes. Lines 1 and 2 show incorrect turn shape. Line 3 shows the correct shape for a series of linked short turns.*

LINE ONE: This shows a very shallow turn pattern barely deviating from the fall line. This type of turn pattern makes it very difficult to control speed because the skis stay too much in the fall line. This track is made by a skier that does not finish his turns.

LINE TWO: This turn goes too straight initially and then hooks sharply at the end of the turn. The straight beginning to this turn generates too much speed, and then the skier must slam on the brakes at the end of the turn creating the hook shape. This type of skier always turns below the fall line (see fig. 12.2, page 90). Most intermediate skiers make this type of skidded turn.

LINE THREE: It is a smooth, continuous, and symmetrical pattern representing the type of controlled turn expert skiers make in a variety of conditions. *This shape remains the same regardless of turn size.*

Which turn shape best describes your skiing? If it is shape #1 or #2 we recommend you try the following short turn drill.

SHORT TURN DRILL: Learn to Turn Really Fast

1. Pick a gentle, wide-open slope with a chair lift running up it.
2. Identify a distance between two or three lift towers.
3. Standing at the beginning of this predetermined distance; begin making a series of short turns, continuing for the entire section you previously identified. **DO NOT SKI NEAR THE LIFT TOWERS.**
4. Count your turns as you ski. Each run try to add more turns in this section.
5. Focus on exerting the same amount of leg extension and flexion force for each turn. Your turns should all feel the same.
6. Rebound off the force created by each turn to speed up your transition.
7. Apply the hip slide technique (page 72 and 73).
8. Keep your turns round by pushing on the front of your skis through the entire arc of the turn.
9. Between turns, when your skis are running flat, practice leg and foot steering to accelerate your direction change.

TIP: Make sure you are in excellent physical condition before attempting this drill. It requires high energy output combined with strong quick, movements of the body.

After mastering the short turn drill on a gentle slope, try it on progressively steeper slopes. Increase your edging pressure on the steeper slopes so that *you travel down the fall line at the same speed here as you did on the gentle slope.* If this is difficult for your to do, you are not finishing your turns. Make sure you complete the turn by applying Continuous Pushing (pressure), on the front of your skis, throughout the whole turn.

If you struggle with this drill return to Chapter 8, Basics of the Carved Turn, for a review. Spend some time repeating the exercises in Part Two and then go back to practicing you short turn drills.

A big mistake many skiers make is trying to improve by spending time on terrain that is beyond their ability. It's a myth that skiing terrain beyond your capabilities will make you a better skier. The fact is you need to put in a lot of practice on easy runs perfecting the fundamentals. Remember those mental/physical engrams? Rehearsing your body position and movement engrams on a regular basis will help immensely. Eventually these new patterns of movement will become automatic. Practicing the fundamentals throughout this book will make you a better skier than most. That is because novice and intermediate skiers never practice the basics, and therefore they never develop a solid foundation. So practice, please. We really want you to have as much fun as we do every time we ski down the mountain.

After practicing short turns are you still having problems? You may have an alignment problem *or poorly tuned skis.* If either or both of these conditions exist you will not be able to make quick round turns in both directions. See Chapter 23 for information about alignment and Chapter 26 to learn about tuning your skis.

TURNING EQUALLY BOTH WAYS

Let's face it; everybody turns better in one direction than the other because our bodies and minds are set up to function asymmetrically. All of us have a dominant side to our bodies: being either left or right handed, having a leg that is longer or weaker, and a brain that science says does certain functions with the right lobe while other duties are handled by the left lobe. But, with all this against us we can still ski symmetrically and at least give the illusion we are turning equally well to the left and right.

Most of us know if we have a weaker turn to one side, but you may not realize how that can hold you back from becoming an advanced all-mountain skier. To identify your weak side think about this; when you start a series of turns, which way do you turn first? Are you comfortable turning in one direction and nervous turning the opposite way? Do you carve your turns more quickly in one direction and then hesitate before you turn back the other direction? Analyze the answers to these questions and you will discover your bad side.

To correct your bad side turn start by identifying the cause. Most likely the problem is rooted in one of two possible areas. You may have a structural deficiency and/or a technical flaw.

Structural problems are based in differences between the left and right side of our bodies, such as one leg being shorter or weaker than the other. Or your body itself may vary from the norm, such as being bowlegged or knock-kneed. You could also be one of the 95% whose feet either pronate (tilt inward) or supinate (tilt outward). An alignment specialist, in conjunction with a good boot fitter, can make adjustments to your equipment in order to correct these structural shortcomings. The important point to remember here is that if you are not correctly aligned in your lower body, it will be much more difficult to balance, and good balance is a very important component of skiing. In fact many professional ski instructors think it is the most important element of expert skiing. For more detail on alignments read Chapter 23 in this book.

A lack of good ski technique will cause a skier to most often compensate with upper body movement. Watch skiers going down the run as you ride up the chairlift. You will soon see skiers that make nice turns in one direction, but they hesitate or struggle during a turn in the other direction. Look closely and you will probably see them do one of the following during their weak side turn: no pole plant, turn their upper body out of the fall line, skid their skis, drop their hand down by their waist, pull their arm across their body, rotate the shoulders in the direction of the turn (as opposed to facing down the hill), and finally traverse too long before turning. Now, what is really amazing is they often do not do any of these things on their strong side turns. All of these technical shortcomings can be correctly easily by keeping your upper body still and facing down the fall line.

It is time to take immediate action and assume the beach ball arm position, face your upper body down the hill during all your turns, and relax. It is always a good idea to practice making symmetrical turns on easier slopes. While practicing, be sure to focus on making equal up and down movements in both turn directions. Trying this will help further identify your weak side turn. At this point, do not let your mind continue to participate in this. You must force your will and command your body to do the CPCPU equally in both directions. Stay with it and continue to practice on an easy slope until you feel a more rhythmic and balanced flow created by turning equally well to both sides.

With less speed and a smooth surface under you it enables you to observe what your body does differently from one turn to the next. If you are still having trouble with the weak side, have a friend stand well below you and make a video recording of your skiing. In most cases nothing motivates more than a good dose of reality. Study the video in slow motion and watch for differences in your weak side and strong side turns. If you identify a technique deficiency, take a refresher course on the correct upper body positions from Part One of this book. Freeze in the beach ball arm position and leave it never more. Oh, and face down hill with a relaxed "teacup" style grip on your poles.

CHAPTER 13

PSUEDO SUPERCARVING (without the Special Gear)

The latest generation of high speed skiers takes a new approach to their fun. They are the supercarvers; a group that carves high edge angle turns down a well-groomed slope, leaving behind only a set of thin lines formed from the skis' edges. Due to recent developments in ski and binding technology these supercarvers can lay down their pure rail-like lines with the precision of a surgeon. The tracks these skiers leave in the snow are precise, narrow, and unvarying. The secret of these carvers lies in their ability to utilize the outside edge of the uphill ski as they carve turns using a modern two-footed technique.

Supercarving is accomplished using shorter shape skis (think 165cm), produced specifically for carving, in combination with carving plates that raise the bindings high off the ski. These plates help the skier exert more leverage on the ski to achieve higher edge angles. Supercarvers are always turning, and it is a sight to behold. You have probably seen them coming down the slope quickly moving from turn to turn as their skis ride a much longer arc around the turn than the skier herself does. These skiers always have their hips far to the inside of the turn. Their body gives the appearance of leaning at an extreme angle during every turn. But, actually it is only their legs that are at this angle and their upper body, or more specifically their shoulders, always remain level or parallel to the slope.

They are using extreme side to side hip movement and hip angulation (see Fig.13.1, page 101) to move their upper body down the hill, and far to the inside of the developing turn. This type of movement will put your ski edges up on an extreme angle. It also often appears that these skiers are diving into their turns, helping both skis to tip high up on their edges and cut a clean tight arc in the snow.

Yes, both skis are significantly on edge, and this is because the skier must carry much more weight on the inside ski to support the body as it tilts more than normal toward the inside of the turn. The weight distribution on their skis approaches 50/50, as opposed to 80% on the downhill ski and 20% on the uphill ski that is used for everyday cruising on the groomed runs.

Another secret to their carving success is their stance. Supercarving skiers typically stand on their skis with their feet farther apart than the rest of us. All of us can experience this sensation of supercarving to some extent while riding on our normal gear. I call this *Pseudo Supercarving*. To get a sense for how it feels to be a supercarver try the following:

PSUEDO SUPERCARVING DRILL

1. Start on an easy and newly groomed slope.
2. Face diagonally across the slope at a slight downward angle.
3. Keep yourself from moving forward by bracing against your poles, which should be positioned out in front of you.
4. Stand with your skis about 24 inches apart.
5. Slide your hips in the uphill direction past your uphill ski.
6. Notice that now your downhill leg is stretched out, but not straight.
7. Without changing your position, push off moving diagonally across the hill.
8. Your downhill ski will bite into the snow as you make a slow gradual turn.
9. Before long your turn should take you uphill a bit and you can stop.
10. Repeat what you just did going in the other direction.
11. Each time you do these continue to slide your hips in the uphill direction.
12. Next begin linking some slow turns, on gentle terrain, using this technique. Remember to keep your feet wider apart than usual, but not so far apart that it makes you unstable or causes discomfort. Slide your hips laterally into each turn.
13. If you become comfortable with this drill you can gradually increase the speed. You will need to move your hips from side to side more quickly as speed increases.

TIP: Do not rotate or turn your hips, only slide them side to side.

Figure 13.1 *Pseudo Supercarving.* *This shows the elements of carving tight arcs on the groomed runs. Notice the high edge angles combined with the wide stance leading to hips that are placed well to the inside of the turn. Weight distribution is 50/50 on the skis and the shoulders are parallel to the slope angle. The legs still remain close together!*

It will take time and practice before you will be ripping off those fast, tight super carves. It is important to note here that the high speed supercarvers you see on the slopes have taken years to develop their skills. So be patient and work on sliding your hips further to the inside of the turn at a faster and faster rate, until you begin to feel a sensation of diving from the uphill side of turn into the downhill side of the next turn. Your skis will come around fast, enabling you to stay on your feet and enjoy the ride. Some skiers enjoy supercarving so much they no longer do anything else. The simply exist to supercarve on the groomers.

This may or may not happen to you, but before you run out and buy a supercarving setup you may want to demo a pair if you can find them. This might be difficult to do locally, but if you are on your way to a major resort you can call ahead and reserve a pair.

How Much Weight on each Ski?

By now you know how I just can't resist a good digress, so just be a little more patient and I will give you the last few pieces of the puzzle needed before we leave the groomed slopes and head for the powder. One puzzle piece that is often ignored is assigning percentages to the amount of weight that ends up on the inside and outside skis during turns in different kinds of snow. This is a tad bit nebulous but I think we can throw some numbers at it, and give you a good ballpark feel for what is happening.

On the following chart, D stands for Downhill ski, U represents the Uphill ski, and the corresponding numbers next to the letters represent the percentage of your total body weight that is on that particular ski. We have included this chart only as a reference point so that we can all have an understanding of the weight distribution on the uphill and downhill skis in different kinds of snow.

This chart does reveal two interesting points. It shows that there are only subtle differences in weight distribution per ski on the various types of snow. But there is a trend in these numbers. You can see Crud and Powder require a more even weight distribution, while Steeps are best skied with more weight on the downhill ski. Groomed runs are an animal on to themselves, and this is the only type of snow where you have a very wide range of choices for weight distribution. Simply put, groomed runs are easy to ski even if your technique is a bit questionable. This is not an excuse to be lazy about your weight transfers and edge sets on groomed snow. Instead it is an opportunity for you to practice loading your skis with different weight distributions. You will benefit from skiing groomed runs as you vary the amount of weight on each ski. This is a great exercise as it allows you to feel the difference between turning with 90% of your weight on the downhill ski versus turning with 60% of your weight on the downhill ski and so on.

The approximate percentages shape up like this:

Type of snow condition	Beginning your run	Initiating each turn	Pressure through turn	Comments
Groomed		D80 –U20	D80-U20	Be patient & ride through a clean arc.
Crud	Depends on severity of crud	D65-U35	D65-U35	Image your knees are tied together with a belt, but can still move up and down independently.
Moguls	D70-U30 Half turn to start.	D60-U40	D50-U50 at the end of turn	Start each run w/ half turn to a check to energize skis.
Steeps	Start slow	D90-U10	D75-U25	Ski in control with strong edge sets.
Powder	Cautious first half turn to get a feel for the snow	D60-U40	D55-U45	Glue knees together (not literally)
Super Carve		D50 - U50 To Learn: Start w/ 70/30	D50 – U50	You feel like you are riding on rails.

I love a good chart, as it often becomes a catalyst for heated debate among aficionados of a particular subject matter. And this chart will create debate as to its correctness, its worthiness, and probably even its layout. However, before the debate begins, I want to make one solid point in defense of this chart. I reviewed these numbers with two ex-world class skiers, three ski instructors, and two expert recreational skiers in order to arrive at these numbers. I guess the moral of the story is: Even if this chart deviates from the perceived norm, it still gives you numbers that you can rely on to help you become an expert skier. For our purposes, these numbers are very accurate and I believe that even the people who would debate their accuracy would in the end only make slight adjustments to them. Carry on!

CHAPTER 14

POWDER: A Safe Fearless Approach

Skiing powder is just not that hard. Most skiers' anxiety about skiing powder stems from not recognizing that they need to do just a few things differently. You cannot approach powder using the same techniques you use to ski groomed slopes. Because powder has a softer and more fluid consistency than packed snow, it is imperative that you use a specific set of techniques to account for this difference. Let's start by making a list of what you need to do to ski powder effectively, and then we can talk about each one individually.

Tips and Techniques for Good Powder Skiing

1. **Use All-Mountain or Powder Skis.**
2. **Start with the Half Turn to a Check.**
3. **Ski With Your Knees Glued Together.** (not literally), and never let those legs come apart.
4. **Use Speed and Pressure to Turn in Powder.** You need to be a bit more aggressive in powder.
5. **Stay Centered Fore and Aft On Your Skis.** Do not sit back!
6. **Distribute Your Weight (More) Evenly Over Both Skis.** Place 55 - 60% of your weight on the outside ski. With your skis weighted more evenly you create a platform to ski on.
7. **Become an Advanced Powder Skier.**

Discussing these elements separately will allow you to see how each contributes to creating a great foundation for powder skiing. Doing these seven things correctly is all it takes for you to shred powder. It is total fun, but you must be like Dorothy in the *Wizard of Oz*: You have to believe you can do it (skiing powder that is; not getting back to Kansas). Allow these seven tips to take you to the realm of the expert powder skier. Clicking your heels together; however, won't be necessary. To help you become a successful powder skier, we will supply you with some magic of our own at the end of this chapter. It is a list of tips on how to safely ski powder, enabling you to learn without fear.

Figure 14.1 *The authors doing laps in the backcountry.*

1. Use All-Mountain or Powder Skis

I will say no more! Well, just a little more, because I want you to enjoy the experience and come back for more (powder skiing that is). Frankly, life in the powder is easiest if you ski on a powder specific ski. No other ski will offer as much floatation or confidence inspiring security like an extra-wide powder ski. However, if just can't afford or just don't want to create a quiver of specialized skis, then you can use an all-mountain ski; also a great performer in powder. You will discover that the newest all-mountain skis are capable of turning like a slalom ski, yet they float nicely in powder and are at home in the crud as well. Just remember the fatter the ski the less resistance you will encounter from the snow. Fat = Float, not sink. Rent a pair of fat skis on your next powder day and you will sing out gleefully as you cut through the freshies (ski speak meaning powder).

2. Start with the Half Turn to a Check

We discussed this turn in Chapter 12, on pages 91 and 92. You will remember it is the *half turn* used to begin each series of turns in all snow conditions. At the start of your next powder run, push off with your skis pointing straight down hill. Let them run until the tips float up a bit, and then quickly move to the check turn to energize (or load) your skis. Trust us, making your first turn in powder a half turn is much easier than trying to start with a complete turn. As you do this check turn, you will get some feedback about the depth and density of the snow. In denser snow, the resistance under your ski will build up more quickly, meaning you will need to push harder on your skis to control them through the turn.

In powder, make your check turn by applying increasing pressure downward, with the most force or push coming at the end of the check turn. Don't just unload both guns as you would while making a big hockey stop; however, or you will fly over your skis like Superman launching out of a window. The problem is you can't fly, and you will just bury your face in the snow. A check turn is not a hockey stop, yet it is similar in shape. Create just enough force at the end of the check turn to rebound off it and transition into your first full turn. Developing a feel for just how much force you should use takes practice, so don't despair if your first few attempts aren't perfect. Take it easy and try to feel the pressure build under your skis as the snow pushes back on them.

To help you start with a great check turn you need to gather some preliminary information on the condition of the snow. Applying a little trick we use before skiing a powder run does this. Prior to dipping into what appears to be fluffy new powder, we like to slap it with our pole basket to see if it is actually powder, and if it is dense, fluffy, or somewhere in between. This slap of the pole basket will also tell you how deep the powder is, or if the snow is wind crusted, and not powder at all. That is excellent feedback!

If the powder is only a few inches deep you can still make turns with the outside ski bearing most of the weight, but as it gets deeper your legs must move together as a unit, like skiing on a platform (fig. 14.3, page 109). This means you need to apply pressure to the inside ski as well, changing your weight distribution between your skis to around 60% on the downhill ski, and 40% on the uphill ski.

If entering into powder at the top of the run is a bit too un-nerving, try it near the bottom of the run. Find powder next to a groomed run and enter it by traversing straight across the slope a short ways. Your entry should be just far enough from the bottom of this powder section to allow you two or three turns. You will now be standing side-ways on the hill, in the powder. But, this most likely will pose no problem as you can get your skis facing directly down the hill by using the "Half Turn to Begin" technique you learned from this book on page 91 and 92, illustrated in Figure 12.3. Getting your skis pointed downhill, using this "ski-tails-in-the-snow" technique is the easy way to start your powder practice runs.

It works like this; in soft snow, lift one ski up and drive the tail back into the slope behind you. As you drive the tail into the snow your ski tip should be pointing up slightly. Continue to sink the ski tail until your boot stops the ski. Repeat this motion with the other ski and you are now facing downhill with the front of your skis sticking out of the snow. You may have to work your skis sideways, one direction or the other, until they face directly down the hill. You are now ready to use your "Half Turn to Check" technique to start the run.

Figure 14.2 *Starting a Set of Turns in Powder. Dig your skis into the hill behind you with your tips pointing slightly up. This enables you to start straight down the fall line and use the Half Turn to Begin maneuver.*

After you become comfortable with making a few turns in the powder, you can move further up the hill and increase to five or six turns per set. Remember to set up your turns, so that you finish the powder run by skiing onto a groomed slope.

3. Knees Glued Together

Before you begin your next powder run, stop at the top and think about holding your legs tightly against each other. Press your knees together and flex your ankles back and forth to get the feel of moving up and down with your legs held closely together. Keeping your legs and feet right next to each other at all times in the powder ensures that you ski on a single platform, as compared to being on two independent skis.

Think of this platform as a flexible piece of semi-rigid plastic that will allow your feet to make slight up and down movements independent of each other, but will not allow your feet to separate side to side. Often, ineffective powder skiers have problems controlling their skis because they are skiing on them independently, and in many cases they are doing just what they do on firmer snow; putting significantly more weight on the outside ski, or simply skiing with their legs too far apart.

Figure 14.3 *Powder Ski on a Semi-Rigid Platform: Ski as if your skis can not be separated. Use a 60/40 weight split, with 60% of your weight on the downhill or outside ski. Never allow the legs to separate side to side. A small amount of independent up and down leg action is ok.*

When your skis act independently they usually behave badly in powder. One ski may dive down as the other one climbs to the surface and the skis can easily cross. Too much weight on one ski can cause you to turn sharply, rotating your upper body out of the fall line, and down you go. In powder, instead of skiing with an outside ski dominant stance, you move to a more even weight distribution between your skis.

There is an element of risk to all types of skiing, but you can practice the "knees glued together" technique in a relatively safe environment. Visit a ski area familiar to you, and pick a short blue or green slope with fresh powder on it. The run should not have trees, bushes, rocks, or cliffs on it. It is best to find a powder-covered slope *bordering a groomed run,* so if you get uncomfortable you can return to easier terrain. Stand at the top of this slope, hold your legs together, ski straight down until your skis float up a bit, and then begin turning. Stay centered over your skis. Don't react to little bumps and jostles feeding back to you from your skis. Stay the course, with legs together and make turns. If you feel yourself a bit in the back seat, move your hands forward in the beach ball position and you will stabilize over your skis. Relax in a big way, and float through the snow practicing CPCPU with close to equal weight on both skis. It will work, and you can do it!

4. Use Speed and Pressure to Turn in Powder.

Control in powder skiing is derived from turning your skis. As you know by now, when you apply pressure to your skis they bend, and the more they bend, the tighter they turn. How much your skis bend is directly related to how hard you pressure or push on them. But in powder skiing, you must first use speed to build pressure under your skis. Just remember, the more speed you carry the more your skis will plane up on the snow.

As your speed increases in powder the snow particles are passing under your skis at a faster rate. This creates a denser snow layer for your skis to ride on and pushes them toward the surface. Control comes from a combination of speed and applying pressure down onto the ski during the turn.

The correct combination creates a powder turn that forms a shallower arc than on groomed snow, resulting in a less than perfect half circle. Looking at Figure 14.1 on page 106, you will see the powder tracks in the photo show each turn at a 45 degree angle to the fall line. The turns look like a series of linked "Z's" tilted to the side at 45 degrees. They are shaped this way because expert powder skiers accelerate by staying closer to the fall line. This allows the skis to float up in the first half of the turn, and creates pressure under them. It is an easier turn to make in powder, unlike the round half circle turn you would carve on firmer snow.

Finding the right combination of speed and pressure is the tricky part. If you put too much pressure on your skis in the beginning of the turn, you go too slow and you auger deep into the snow by the end of the turn. The same thing can also happen if you are going too fast coming into the second half of the turn. In this situation, novice powder skiers often apply too much pressure at the end of the turn in an attempt to quickly slow down. This causes the skis to sink, and it usually results in a complete stop and/or fall.

Be subtle and patient as you develop your turns. If you start with just a little pressure and your skis are not turning quickly enough to slow you down, stay with it and push harder to make the ski finish the turn. Think of it like this: *Applying increasing pressure throughout the turn is the secret to great powder skiing.* Leaving the turn too soon develops too much acceleration.

Often, this pushes you onto the back of your skis. Skiing in the back seat is the worst thing you can do in powder. That is not how you get your tips to come up.

But, how do you know when you are going fast enough? Not to worry; as you begin a powder run, you *will not* need to stay in the fall line very long. It will only be a second or two before your skis begin to float up. Be sure to stay centered on your skis, fore and aft, and wait for the float. As speed increases so does the resistance under your skis, causing them to move toward the surface. Be brave here, and patiently resist the urge to turn or sit back on your skis. If you stay centered you will feel your skis come up, and at that moment you will make your *half turn* to load the skis. Then you can just modulate your speed by increasing or decreasing the pressure you exert on your skis through the second half of each consecutive turn.

To increase the pressure on your skis flex your ankles forward, thus pressing harder on the front of your boot cuffs. This will tighten your turn causing your skis to come across the fall line at a sharper angle and slow you down. To increase your speed in powder simply release some of the pressure off the front of your boot cuff by straightening you legs a little bit. This action elongates your turn and decreases the resistance on your skis allowing you to speed up. Finally, turn equally to both sides to create a rhythm and stick to it.

5. Stay Centered on Your Skis

We have talked about how important it is for your upper body to remain quiet and this applies in powder skiing as well. Any gross movement of the upper body wreaks havoc on your skiing when the snow is firm, and in powder this is amplified even more causing you to lose your balance and fall. Need we say more? Powder, being so fluid and soft, offers no foundation upon which to regain your balance.

To avoid this, you must stay centered (fore and aft) over your skis by keeping you arms in the correct position: chest high and wide spread with your palms facing each other and your elbows held up. Of course, this is exactly the position your arms would be in if you were holding a large **beach ball** against your chest, as illustrated in Chapter 3 Figure 3.1 on page 24. Keeping your arms spread wide and out in front of you is the single most important thing you can do to stay centered over your skis. What is the second most important thing? In our humble opinion, it is keeping your hips centered over your feet. This is best accomplished by flexing your ankles forward, never allowing your butt to drop behind your heels. Stand up on your skis, with your ankle flexed a bit and try to avoid leaning against the back of your boots. But, if you do, just smoothly and quickly thrust your arms out in front of you.

6. Distribute Your Weight More Evenly Over Both Skis

Many people (including professionals) say you should distribute your weight evenly over both skis in powder, and it works. But, it is just a bit more complicated, depending on the surface, or lack there of, under the powder you are skiing. The following list will give you some guidelines for weighting each ski in different types of powder, where D is for downhill ski and U is for uphill ski. If that is confusing, just remember that the downhill ski is also the outside ski at the end of the turn, and conversely the uphill ski is always the inside ski at the end of the turn.

> **1. A few inches of powder on a firm base of snow: D70/U30.**
> **2. Knee deep powder with no base under it: D60/U40.**
> **3. Thigh deep powder and beyond: D55/U45.**

Powder skiing is still outside ski dominant. Good skiers are shifting more weight to the outside ski, although the weight transfer is more subtle and less forceful than on firmer snow. However, beginning powder skiers are far too outside ski dominant, meaning they put much more weight on the downhill ski in a turn. This happens because the centrifugal force you develop in the turn is always trying to throw you to the outside. You naturally resist this force by pushing back with your outside ski to avoid catapulting downhill. To further illustrate this, imagine you are standing on a slope, with a person above you and that person decides to shove you. You will resist by placing one leg down the hill to brace against the force of the shove.

To stop your desire to primarily weight the outside ski in powder, you must voluntarily push on the inside ski and outside ski at the same time with close to equal pressure. This is easy to do because you will involuntarily weight the outside or downhill ski just like you always do, meaning you will only need to think about pressuring your inside ski. To do this, use your leg muscles to voluntarily push down on the inside ski.

If you have trouble weighting the inside ski during your powder turns, there is an exercise you can do to learn this skill. It was developed by a world cup racer and it quickly teaches you what it feels like to put significant weight on your inside ski. It is the stepping-stone to weighting both skis more equally through the turn. The drill unfolds as follows:

Inside Ski Dominant Turns: On-Snow Drill

1. As always, find a nice groomed beginner or intermediate slope.
2. Pick a safe place to practice traversing.
3. Traverse across the hill with your weight on the uphill (outside) edge of the uphill ski. Keep your arms wide, using your poles for balance.
4. Reverse the traverse, and use the other uphill (outside) edge of the uphill ski to come back across the slope. Do this a few times to get comfortable.
5. Now begin to link some turns using only the outside edge of the inside ski to carve (fig. 14.4.) Put most of the weight on this inside ski and weight the downhill ski only enough to stay in balance.
6. Be cautious, taking care not to catch an edge and fall.

This exercise teaches you to keep more weight on your inside ski, and it will immediately make powder skiing easier because you now understand what it feels like to weight the inside ski in a turn, as well as the outside ski. Focus on the feeling of skiing on the outside edge of your inside ski, and try to mimic this feeling the next time you are in the powder. But, unlike in the exercise, you will also have weight on your downhill ski. You have now learned how to weight both skis and create your platform for skiing powder.

Figure 14.4 *Ski on the Outside Edge of the Inside Ski. The skier on the left is skiing on the outside edge of the inside ski. The skier on the right is doing the opposite, and skiing as everyone typically does, with the weight on the inside edge of the downhill ski. When talking about weighting the skis, the skier on the left is inside ski dominant, and the skier on the right is outside ski dominant.*

SIMPLY PUT: CARVE ON YOUR INSIDE SKI, NOT YOUR OUTSIDE SKI. For a few runs try being inside ski dominant, meaning you are skiing with most of your weight on your inside ski. Be careful, because if you catch your edge in this drill you can fall downhill, slamming into the snow with more force than the usual fall to the uphill side.

7. Become an Advanced Powder Skier

You do not have to master the following powder skiing skill in order to have fun in all types of powder. Just do the six things we talked about throughout this chapter and you will do fine. But, if you want to take it to the next level, then this is what you can do to learn to ski powder with the experts.

You will need to *up un-weight* to power your skis through the turn. This is contrary to all the "up and down" we have talked about in the book, but it works great for powder. We have been telling you to compress your knees to load the ski and power it through the turn. Now you will still flex your knees, but this time you will be pulling them up under you from an extended leg position; literally tucking them up under your upper body. Make sense? With the upward motion of your knees you are literally un-weighting you skis. You are yanking your body weight right off your skis. Try the following exercise to get a feel for up un-weighting.

Powder Skiing On-Snow Drill

1. Pick an untracked section of a *moderate, short* slope.
2. Traverse across the slope bouncing up and down, while standing tall.
3. Create the bounce by pulling your feet upward in gentle, short jumps. (many ski instructors compare this to jumping rope at school)
4. Focus on staying in balance and centered over your skis as you jump.
6. When you reach the speed at which your skis start to plane on the snow your bouncing will be almost effortless. The jump height is just a few inches.
7. Now, take this skill to a section of powder where you can make turns.
8. **Secret Tip:** Before you push off make sure you are holding your legs tightly together. Concentrate on this the entire run. Do not let your legs drift apart.
9. Distribute your weight on two skis. 60% downhill, 40% uphill (feels like 50/50.)
10. Remember to start with a straight run (until skis float) to a half turn.
11. Bounce off this half turn into a full turn. Be sure to flex your legs upward, as if jumping rope, to transition into the next turn. Apply just enough pressure in the turn to control your speed. You should be applying the most pressure at the end of the turn.

What you do next will help with this up un-weighting concept. To power your skis into a powder turn, you extend your legs down into the snow to load or pressure them. You can vary how far you sink in the snow by how aggressively you extend your legs down into it. To modulate your speed, you will need a combination of downward pressure and pointing of the knees. This turning technique replaces a good portion of hip angulation, because you can not generate enough force from the soft surface under your skis to support dropping you hip deep into the turn (the hole). You may refer to Figure 10.4 on page 78 for a refresher on hip angulation and dropping into the hole. You ski powder with a more upright stance. Look at the skier in the Figure 14.1 photograph on page 106. He is standing tall, with almost no hip angulation apparent. And, I can personally attest that he did not fall or miss a turn on this day.

The secret to up un-weighting in powder lies in never moving your upper body. It does not lift *up* to un-weight your skis. Your knees do it; they pull your legs up which releases your skis from the downward pressure you have been using to ride through the turn. With your skis un-weighted you extend your legs to load the skis and point your knees toward the direction you want to turn. Extend your legs strongly down and you make a tight short turn, coming across the fall line at a sharper angle. Extend your legs with lighter force, and your turn becomes longer, causing you to deviate less from the fall line. Your hips always remain about the same distance from the snow and your legs "work like pistons" under your upper body. See Figure 14.5.

Figure 14.5 *Keep Hips on a Plane Parallel to the Slope. Contrary to common belief, when skiing powder you do not lift your upper body up and down with you arms. Your legs flex up to un-weight the skis, and then extend down to form the turn. The upper body remains quiet as usual. The distance between your hips and the snow never changes (strange sounding, but true).*

Tips for Making Powder Skiing Easy

- ✓ Apply the most pressure to your skis at the end of the turn.
- ✓ Vary the pressure on your skis to control your speed. Apply a lot of pressure and you turn more across the fall line and slow down. Apply less pressure and you ski more directly down the fall line at a higher speed.
- ✓ Ski in a rhythm, making smooth turns, avoiding rapid or harsh movements.
- ✓ Use fat skis designed to ski powder.
- ✓ Work your legs as a single unit. Together they flex (or jump) up out of the turn, and then extend down into the turn. This is up un-weighting.
- ✓ Extending your legs deeper into the snow will slow you down.
- ✓ Extending your legs gently into the snow (using less force) will allow you to speed up.
- ✓ Extending your legs with a lot of force at the end of the turn makes you turn sharper. Not always a good thing, but it can rapidly slow you.
- ✓ Don't turn completely across the hill, because making a turn from a traverse is more difficult.
- ✓ Ski on a platform created by your skis.
- ✓ Weight your skis more evenly. 60/40, 55/45, or 50/50. It's all good.
- ✓ Start your run with a short ride straight down the fall line to allow your skis to float up before making your half turn to start.
- ✓ Never sit back. Stay centered, fore and aft, over your skis.
- ✓ Relax, and ride all the way through the turn, don't panic and hockey stop to your face.
- ✓ If, after all else fails and your skis still won't float – get fatter skis.
- ✓ Still can't float? Make sure you are aligned fore and aft in your boots correctly. Too much forward lean will make you a habitual auger-person (right down into the snow.) See Chapter 23 on alignment.
- ✓ Throw your boots away if they are too stiff flexing forward.

DIGRESSION

The fact is that using the ankles is part of skiing like an expert, and if you can't easily flex your boot forward, you can't use them effectively. How do you know if your boots are too stiff? I suggest you tighten your bottom two buckles and loosen the upper two buckles a little and see if this helps your skis float up in powder. For that matter, start by skiing a few groomed runs and see if your turns come easier, with less time spent against the back of your boots.

WHAT TIP WOULD THE BEST POWDER SKIERS GIVE YOU?

We hear a lot of great tips on skiing powder. One of our favorites has a real flair for the obvious. "You can't improve unless you practice." Because powder is somewhat elusive, a sure way to catch up with the fluffy stuff is spend a week heli-skiing, or invest in a day with a snowcat operation. These operations usually supply you with fat powder skis, and they will sign you up even if you are a novice. Be honest, and talk to them about how they handle aspiring powder skiers.

Whether you spend the big bucks to get your powder, or you search it out on your own; our friend Mark has a tip you can use. He is arguably one of the best powder skiers in the Pacific Northwest. When he gets going in the powder he exhibits that unmistakable pumping action in his legs, while his upper body appears motionless.

We asked Mark to tell us his secret to skiing deeper powder. This is the kind of powder snow that builds up over several days, from one or more large storms.

The following paragraphs capture his comments in his own words:

Most people don't realize that the same rhythm they use to make turns on a groomed slope does not work in powder. Your skis meet with greater resistance in deep powder, especially when turning through multi-layered snow media. As a result, your ski takes longer to come around in the turn. Your turn radius will be the same in both situations, it just takes the ski longer to complete the turn in powder, because the resistance created by the snow slows your forward movement.

In addition, it takes time for the skis to compress the snow below the surface in order to create a "platform" for the skis to load up against, before you can rebound into the next turn. Aspiring powder skiers, not realizing this, want to turn before the ski is ready. They are relying on the same turn rhythm that works for them on the groomers, when making consecutive short turns. But, in powder, your everyday turn cadence will fail you until you add patience.

When it is deep, you must wait until the ski starts to plane out of the snow before you initiate the next turn. This is similar to a water skier getting up on one ski. To do it successfully the water skier waits for the ski to plane up on the water before standing up (patience.) On snow, the ski rounds out the turn as the tip floats closer to the surface. This creates a different rhythm than the one you are accustomed to feeling on firmer snow. Be patient and let the turns fully develop. If you carry speed down

the hill, and move slower through the turn you will get awesome results. It's an oxymoron, but it works. (Mark is pictured below)

CHAPTER 15

MOGUL SKIING MADE EASY

This section contains valuable information about the basics of mogul skiing, but is somewhat limited in scope. We have chosen to take this approach because we know that mogul skiing requires an entire book to adequately cover the subject. To that end, we have created a Mogul E-booklet:

A Weekend Warrior's Guide to Mogul Skiing Technique
Available now at weekendwarriorsguide.com!

Incredibly, America's premier mogul skiing family is involved in this E-booklet, and the accompanying DVD download. Every member of the family has been a successful mogul competitor, and Dad was even a world champion. The E-booklet is refreshing in that it teaches you to carve turns in the bumps, creating a look that is smooth and stylish. That's right, you don't have to thump your way straight down the moguls like a bouncing ball, as many young skiers do today. It is possible to make round, carved turns in the moguls and still ski fast. Making carved turns in the moguls is easy on your body, looks fabulous, and gives you the highest level of control possible. In addition, this E-booklet offers tips on choosing the right equipment and skiing every type of mogul, from icy to packed powder. Look for it on our website, weekendwarriorsguide.com, by August of 2008. You will be glad you did.

Remarkably, there is a plethora of written information available on skiing Moguls, yet doing it correctly remains one of great unsolved mysteries to most skiers. Let's start by unraveling the mystery a bit. The first notion to address is what correct mogul skiing should look like. For young, strong, competitive mogul skiers; it usually looks like a straight down, high-speed descent in the "zipper line or "ruts" between the bumps. This type of skier does not make carved turns in the traditional sense, or keep their skis on the snow. To ski like this you need both the desire and the ability to endure a lot of shock from slamming into the bumps, and the injuries that more frequently accompany this style of mogul skiing.

For the rest of us, it should look like a fall line descent consisting of round turns, linked one after the other, in a rhythmic succession of carved arcs. Knowing how to carve your turns in the moguls will enable you to make quiet and beautiful turns in the fall line no matter how steep it becomes. I am just saying it looks better and hurts less, so why not do it. Also, you will have much more control.

People often want to know the secret to mogul skiing, and I respond by telling them it lies in creating a strong foundation of basic skiing techniques. Yes, the same techniques you use to ski on groomed runs are, for the most part, the same skills needed to ski bumps. Having a poor understanding of the fundamentals will make mogul skiing very difficult. This is because when you make a mistake in the bumps you do not have the luxury of spending whatever time it takes to correct the mistake. On a groomed run mistakes happen, and you have plenty of time and room to get back in control by slowing down or stopping.

Struggling mogul skiers display a few common types of descent patterns that do not show up on the groomed runs: go fast – then crash, go fast – hang on to the bottom, or the "linked traverses" style of getting down the hill. A skier that can only descend the moguls by traversing back and forth must cross the fall line path of fast mogul skiers, endangering everyone. The bummer happens when the *go fast-then crash* fall line skier engages the *linked traverse style* skier.

Figure 15.1 *Sitting Back with Arms held Low and Close to the Body.* *When the arms drop down it pushes the skier into the back seat, and he is unable to weight the front of the skis to control the turn. This results in unwanted acceleration and loss of control. His hips are positioned behind his heels, instead of centered over his feet.*

To avoid this scenario you need to spend time doing your homework before you head to the moguls for exciting fall line skiing. The prerequisites that will prepare you are the beach ball arm position with the teacup grip, and a correct body position. In addition, you must be proficient at making rhythmic short radius turns on a groomed run. Master these skills and it is time to take it to the moguls. But, before you point 'em down famous mogul runs like The Plunge or Exhibition, you will need to add several new techniques specific to mogul skiing. The key to success is having a set of tools you can remember and apply in a safe and un-intimidating environment. That is the challenge we will address for each tip and technique listed below. Whoops! I better confess, the first item on this list is somewhat of a review.

Tips and Techniques for Good Mogul Skiing

1. **Apply the Basic Fundamentals of Skiing.**
2. **Keep your Feet Together and Move the Legs in Unison.**
3. **Look Ahead to Proactively Ski Moguls.**
4. **Ski in the Ruts as a Beginning Technique.**
5. **Absorb, then Extend (It's the secret.)**
6. **Use a Special Pole Plant in the Moguls.**
7. **Learn to Ski the Sides of Moguls.**
8. **Learn to Ski the Tops of Moguls.**
9. **Turning in Moguls is a Mixed Bag.**
10. **Avoid the "Thump a Bump" by Carving your Turns.**
11. **How to Safely Ski the Bumps.**
12. **Does Equipment Make a Difference?**

1. Apply the Basic Fundamentals of Skiing

It is no surprise that all good mogul skiers stay in control. They have mastered the fundamental skills necessary to ski moguls. For most experts, this is accomplished by utilizing a formal approach to learning their sport, with a strong focus on the basics such as hand position, body position, and lower body action.

A poor positioning of body parts is usually why ineffective mogul skiers cannot control their speed. As a result they are often victims of the *three turns and you're out* rule. This means that after three turns they're out of control and headed for the sidelines, or in this case, the side of the run. Typically, this happens because ineffective skiers have their hands out of position, their feet are too far apart, they are too far forward or back, and/or they do not properly extend their legs down the back side of each mogul. A quick review of chapters one and two of this book may be in order to make sure you have each body position and movement embedded in your muscle memory and your mind. Are they engrams yet?

2. Keep Your Feet Together and Move the Legs in Unison

In the moguls your feet, legs, and skis need to work together doing things in the same place at the same time. Events happen fast here, and a narrow stance is a huge advantage when applying mogul skiing technique. For example, a wider stance can put you in the awkward situation of having one ski high on the side of a bump, while the other ski is down in the rut. This will certainly disrupt your rhythm by making your next turn difficult, at the very least. With your legs close together, and working as a single unit, you can more quickly execute the advanced "absorb and extend" mogul skiing technique we will talk about later.

3. Look Ahead to Proactively Ski Moguls

Moguls are not a uniform set of formations that are predictable. In fact, it is just the opposite, as bumps seem to be getting more irregular, rutted, and chopped off every year. This is all the more reason for you to be looking ahead; not just down in front of your skis. Looking ahead a few rows in the moguls gives your mind time to process information about what is coming, and send this data to your muscles. Then, your body has the time to make adjustments for the changing landscape in front of you.

Figure 15.2 *Eyes Look Ahead Two or Three Rows. This allows the skier to adjust for changes in the mogul shapes before hitting them. Looking ahead keeps the head up and helps maintain an erect stance.*

If you see a bump with a big hole or wall where the front side should be, you want to avoid it to keep your run going smoothly. Because all things happen relatively fast in the bumps, you need to see this wall in advance to give yourself time to make an adjustment for it. This adjustment may be in

122

the form of a hop over the hole, or you may alter your line slightly left or right to avoid it. If you are always looking down at the mogul directly in front of you, there will not be enough time to make the necessary adjustments. The net result is you smack the wall or hole, which greatly disrupts your rhythm or causes you to fall.

Eyes Looking Ahead On-Snow Drill

1. Begin by picking a groomed, easy slope to practice on.
2. Locate a focus point down the run about 50 yards. This can be any stationary object such as a tree, sign or small building.
3. Next, make a series of slow turns while keeping your eyes looking at the object. Resist the temptation to look down at your skis.
4. Repeat this until you become comfortable with your skis absorbing the minor irregularities beneath your feet without you looking at them.
5. After you have read this entire section on skiing moguls, find a moderately sloped bump run, and enter it only about ten rows from the end. At first, slowly ski through it looking one or two rows out in front. Trust your skis, for they will absorb the terrain changes (as we will remind you).

NOTE: We recommend you start looking ahead about one or two rows, and as you develop this skill increase it up to three rows.

4. Ski in the Ruts as a Beginning Technique

Right after we explain how you ski the ruts, and you learn to do it, then we want you to stop doing it. That sounds like a waste of time, but it's not. Think of starting in the ruts as a way to easily become comfortable with moguls before you move on to carving turns anywhere but in the ruts. Let's set a goal of making controlled turns straight down the fall line without expending huge amounts of energy. The big deal here is to control your speed, and everything else will fall into place. Speed control is the ticket that will get you ripping through the moguls faster and faster, if you so desire. Just remember, faster skiing in the bumps requires an incredible amount of practice at *slower speeds*. At the very least, speed control will make your skiing in the moguls a relaxed and pleasurable experience, and from that point you can decide where it will take you. But, for now let's talk about how to slow down and enjoy the ride.

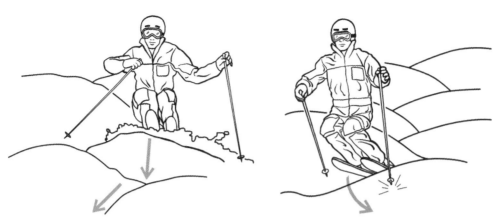

Figure 15.3 *Rut Skiing vs. Carved Turns.* *The skier on the left is skiing fast in the ruts using primarily strong edge checks with an exaggerated "absorb and extend" technique. The skier on the right is standing tall and carving through the bumps, avoiding the ruts most of the time. This skier turns mostly on the white open spaces, not in the ruts. Avoiding the ruts allows you to make a smoother, less jarring descent.*

A key to skiing moguls slowly, or any other way for that matter, is to stand tall. Standing up in the moguls is easy physically, but the reason most aspiring bump skiers have trouble with it stems from their fear of what lies ahead. It is natural for you to be apprehensive about speeding through the moguls, and it is this apprehension that makes you lean back on the tails of your skis or assume a crouched, defensive posture. Both are wrong and actually make it harder to ski because these positions limit your range of motion and control over your skis. So, get centered on your skis and stand tall!

You cannot always turn where and when you want to in the bumps, requiring you to be ready to make slight adjustments to your line of descent. Standing tall *in between each turn* gives you the ability to adjust your legs and upper body as needed, to ski around or over whatever obstacle the next bump may throw at you. However, if you are crouched forward you are already compressed and have lost some of your range of motion, making it very difficult to absorb that really big rut or hole that seemly appears out of nowhere. If you are back on your skis and you launch off a bump unexpectedly, you will be pushed further back and unable to regain control over your skis. Next, you will be launched off the bump in front of you with your ski tips higher than you head. Do we need to guess what the net result of this event is?

124

Phipps in the bumps at Aspen, wearing today's
fashion Faux Pas: a one piece suit and a Pom-Pom hat.

In the beginning, skiing moguls *slowly* goes hand in hand with skiing *small.* A moderately sloped run with small bumps will allow you to learn the first step in high level mogul skiing without undue duress. This first step is referred to as "skiing the ruts" or "the zipper line." This is the exact drill most ski instructors will first teach their pupils, and frankly many would-be mogul skiers never progress past this stage. Unfortunately for them, natural mogul runs are chopped off, deeply rutted, and irregular in size and shape; making skiing the rut line a very difficult proposition (especially as the bumps get bigger and bigger). Don't let that discourage you. These bumps can be skied smoothly.

Beginning mogul skiers find it easier to learn how to ski around the bumps before mastering the more advanced techniques required to ski the tops and sides of the moguls. Skiing in the rut line is a four step process. Begin by skiing down between two bumps and into the bump below you. (1) Just before you reach the lower bump, initiate a check turn or mild hockey stop to scrub speed. (2). Absorb the compression of this check turn by pressing into this lower bump with your legs, flexing forward at the ankles and knees. (3). As you compress into this bump, plant your pole on top of it and rebound off the check turn to a standing position and (4) continue by *sliding* around the side of the bump and down into the next "rut."

Figure 15.4 *Check Turn To Scrub Speed in the Bumps.* *Check speed against the front side of the bumps. Rebound off this check into an elongated stance to release the ski edges. Steer and slide the skis around the mogul, and repeat the slow-down phase using a check turn against the front side of the next mogul.*

You are actually using the shape of the bump to direct your skis around it. Every time you arrive at a new bump you need to make a strong edge set and then rebound off it. This rebound takes you to an upright stance as you ride around the bump, and get ready to compress down into the next bump below you.

Now you should be riding in the ruts all the way down the hill, or something is wrong with my description. Do this moving slowly. In fact, you should be moving just fast enough so you do not stop when you do your edge set (or a partial hockey stop turn) against each bump. Are you remembering to keep your feet together and head up as you look three rows in front of you at all times?

Ok, I will try to explain what I just said in a more concise way:

Start by skiing between two bumps, and then turn (check) down into the bump in front of you. Rebound off this bump and stand up as you ski between the next two bumps and down into the next rut, where you again turn against the bump to scrub speed. Remember to plant your pole at or near the top of every mogul.

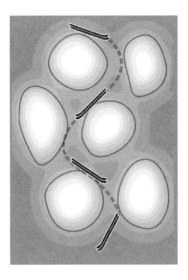

Figure 15.5 *Skiing Around the Bumps in the Rut Line. For beginning mogul skiers, skiing the rut line is the easiest way to get through moderate moguls.*

5. Absorb, then Extend (It's the Secret)

Knowing the ins and outs of absorbing and extending will allow you to master the advanced mogul techniques of making turns on the sides and tops of moguls which we will be discussing later on in this chapter. Being able to use a combination of these turns will make you an expert bump skier. The absorb/extend technique requires that you absorb the bump as you make a hard edge set (check turn) to scrub speed on the front side of the mogul, and then extend your legs down the back side, dropping your ski tips to match the contour of the snow. If you're not getting enough extension, correct it by driving your hips forward as illustrated in Figure 15.6 on the following page.

Coming right up, we will discuss that last paragraph in detail. But, first I feel there is a need to make sure everybody is on the same page. I was recently a bit surprised when I heard an industry professional call the downhill side of a mogul the front face. This is not technically correct from a skier's perspective, and we need to have an accurate description of a mogul so we can communicate. A mogul has a front and a back, which are typically referred to as the front side and the back side. For our purposes here we will be talking about moguls from a point of reference *above* each mogul. Therefore, the front side is what you see first when skiing down to a mogul, and the back is what you arrive at after you ski over the mogul. Not to confuse the issue further, but the left and right of a mogul (looking down the hill) are simply referred to as the "sides."

In Chapter 14 we talked about using up un-weighting to initiate turns through the powder, and some of that same technique applies here in the moguls, with one difference. When you extend your legs down into the next turn you will also need to drop your ski tips down to accept the back side angle of the bump. This is accomplished by pointing your toes downward like a ballet dancer. *This requires hip projection!* Without it you can suffer a variety of maladies as you struggle through the moguls.

Figure 15.6 *Hip Projection. After coming over the top of the bump the hips are pushed forward, the legs are extended, and the ski tips are dropped down to maintain contact with the snow. Point the toes down as the hips drive forward. It's a bit of ballet!*

Lack of hip projection can cause you to be rocked into the back seat, with your butt behind your heels, and you will speed out of control. To avoid this you need to become confident with hip projection and stay centered fore and aft over your skis. Being centered is a very good thing in both skiing and meditation, and it is the nucleus from which all control emanates.

To get centered, you need to extend on the back side of a mogul. Doing it is a two part movement, consisting of both dropping your ski tips down and projecting your hips forward. This helps your skis remain on the snow and places you in a perfect position to absorb the oncoming bump, while you remain centered over your skis. *You cannot be apprehensive about this dual movement!* Yes, you may feel like you are flinging yourself over the tips of your skis, but I can assure you that will not happen. Instead you will enter the realm of control. Here's how you do it.

It all starts with your stance. Skiing the bumps correctly requires you to stand tall on your skis. With your upper body positioned vertically, your legs have a greater range of flexibility for absorbing the bumps. Your upper body needs to be upright and vertical as much as possible when skiing bumps. This means you are standing tall and are centered over your skis, as illustrated on page 40, Figure 6.1. The time to stand tall with your legs extended, is on the back side of the mogul. This prepares you for the next turn sequence in which you begin by making a strong edge set (check) to control your speed on the front side of the mogul. Next, simultaneously release your edges (allowing the skis to turn into the fall line) and absorb the mogul as you go over or around it. Then extend your legs down the back side of the bump. You are now prepared to check at the front of the next mogul, absorb, and then once again, extend your legs down the back of the bump. In other words: Check your speed; absorb the force, and release to a standing position to turn around or over the mogul, and extend. Check/Absorb and Extend, Check/Absorb and Extend, Check/Absorb and Extend, endlessly!

As you ski through the moguls, always make an effort to keep your skis on the snow, unless you need to hop over a small wall that has formed from too many people either slamming on the brakes or traversing in the same place. The subject of hopping will be covered in the upcoming mogul book, as it is a component of higher speed bump skiing. Our goal here is to get you comfortable skiing moderate moguls, and then hand you off to the Weekend Warrior book on mogul skiing where you will learn the most advanced mogul skiing techniques being taught today.

As you look at Figure 15.3 on page 124 notice that the skier on the right actually comes high around the side of the bump, and follows its contour while staying out of the rut. He extends as soon as the bump starts to fall off toward the next rut. Standing tall at this point, with his skis on the snow, prepares him to check speed as he absorbs into the front side of the next bump.

Figure 15.7 *Check Speed, Compress (Absorb) into the Mogul, Extend Down the Back Side. The skier is controlling his speed by checking into the front of the mogul, and then he extends over the back side of the same mogul to elongate his body and prepare for the next turn.*

6. Use a Special Pole Plant in the Moguls

You are already armed with the tools to make a great pole plant in the moguls. Those tools consist of the **beach ball arm** position and the **teacup** grip discussed in Part One. Using just these tools assures your pole plants will be correct. *With your hands wide, palms facing each other, elbows up, and a relaxed grip;* you are easily able to flick the tip of your pole out and make the plant. Do not try to mimic the arm position of competitive bump skiers you see on TV. Often they hold their arms about shoulder width apart. Doing this will greatly slow your progress toward carving turns in the bumps, and right now it will make it difficult for you to keep your hands in front of you and up high. One key to doing this is remembering to never grip your pole tightly with the ring finger and the little finger. This will disable the use of your wrist, which must be used to cock your hand back and then flick out your pole to make each plant. This cock and flick motion is necessary in order to give you the quickness needed to make fast pole plants. You are only moving your wrist, while your hands and arms remain almost stationary. We use the term "almost" because there is a little back and forth movement at the elbow as you extend and retract your poles while planting.

Placement is critical in the moguls, so make sure you always plant out near the tip of your ski. Never plant your pole back at your boots where you can lose sight of your hands. Keep your hands in sight and your skis are much more likely to stay on the snow.

Where you plant your pole is very important and should always occur on or near the top of the mogul. Remember, you are going to flick your pole out in front of you, near your tips as you quickly move from plant to plant. Your pole plant comes at the end of the turn. If you begin a turn and then make your pole plant, your arms will be pulled down and behind you. This is only good if you plan on doing an inadvertent back flip in the moguls.

Things to remember about pole plants in moguls:
1. Flick the pole tip out near the tip of your ski to plant it.
2. After the plant, cock the wrist by swinging *only* it down toward the ground. It is the same wrist motion used to fly cast in fishing. It is a back and forth motion of the wrist. This whips the tip back toward you, and loads your wrist with the energy needed for the next flick of the pole tip.
3. Arms should always be in the beach ball position.
4. Hands use the teacup grip.
5. Palms face each other at all times. If you mistakenly point your palms downhill, your elbows will come in close to your body and your arms will drop back or down. If your knuckles face up hill you are skiing with your palms open to the slope below you. This is bad.
6. Use the right style of pole. It will have a grip that is designed to facilitate flicking the pole tip out in front of you. This type of pole setup is best for all types of skiing and it is discussed extensively in The Equipment Chain section, on pages 194 and 195 of chapter 25.

POLE PLANT SUMMARY: Use the beach ball arm position and teacup grip. Reach out, and flick the wrist forward planting the pole next to your ski tip. Be sure to plant on top of the mogul.

7. Learn to Ski the Sides of Moguls

This is getting into more advanced mogul technique and will be covered completely in the *Weekend Warrior's Guide to Mogul Skiing*. But, we are glad to share just a few comments about adding this technique to your bump skiing arsenal.

If you want to get out of the ruts and ski the sides of bumps, be prepared to speed things up a little. This advanced skill requires the same technique used by racers on a course where the ruts around every gate have deepened due to heavy usage. Essentially you are banking your turns off the sides of the moguls like a racer making turns just above the ruts. This creates a more direct line through the bumps and your speed increases. You will be carving, just like the racer, as you ski over the inside half of each mogul. The one substantial difference is you are standing tall.

Skiing the sides is one more great skill to have at your disposal when trying to avoid deep holes, chopped off bumps, or heinous ruts. The exciting news is this technique allows you to carve every turn when applied correctly. But, that is a subject for another day. Now I bet you can't wait to get the Mogul booklet. Ok, I know it is getting gratuitous to keep mentioning the next Warrior booklet on skiing. Though I am excited about it, I will refrain from mentioning it again, lest it become my bete noire. Then you won't like me.

8. Learn to Ski the Tops of Moguls

This is another weapon for you to add to your bump skiing arsenal. It is especially useful in big bumps with large tops which give you lots of room to make your turns. As you ski the tops of the moguls, a particular sequence of events unfolds. First, you cut across the rut, instead of riding in it or just above it. To be specific, you turn through the rut on the front side of the bumps, and then turn again down the back of the same bump. Imagine that, two turns per bump. And again, you can carve very nice turns doing this, and with practice you may even hear people call out: "You look like a Sun Valley pretty boy skier (or girl)." Hey, it's good to dream.

In this style of mogul skiing, you will definitely be using your absorb and extend skills, as well as your ability to keep your skis on the snow. Skiing the tops is big fun and easy to do as long as you find the right mogul field to practice in. Start on a moderately sloped bump run with soft, forgiving snow conditions. A few inches of new snow on top of packed powder, for example, will give you a pretty nice surface to play on. *Turn on the white open spaces.*

9. Turning in Moguls is a Mixed Bag

Once you have mastered skiing the ruts, sides, and tops of bumps; you can truly be called an expert bump skier. Being able to mix up these three turns in the moguls allows you to ski a more consistent line straight down the run. This is because you now have different techniques for the different situations you will run into along the way.

We always try to pick a good line for our mogul runs, but all we are really doing is scoping out our first handful of turns, and then we need to bring these different techniques to the table to make a smooth run, staying in the fall line all the way down. Knowing how to make these different types of turns in the bumps allows a skier to react to terrain changes more spontaneously and keep the run going, which is very handy in today's moguls, as they are often irregular and ill shaped because of the newer ski profiles.

Since the introduction of shorter, more shaped skis, the holes (ruts) have become more pronounced due to the tails of these skis hitting or digging in at the end of a turn. The flared ski tails lock a skier into the turn, causing their skis to dig in more, actually creating a deep hole below many moguls. Recently, new ski designs are incorporating a more turned up tail which slightly diminishes this digging action in the ruts. The older narrower skis allowed you to release out of the turn earlier creating nice round bumps that a person could easily ski around. Not to worry though, it is still possible to make quick and elegant carved turns through the moguls. Get the book.

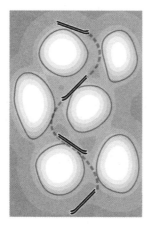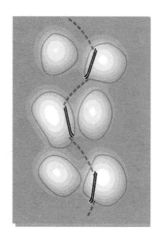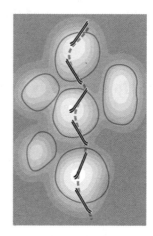

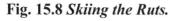

Fig. 15.8 *Skiing the Ruts.*　　　*The Sides.*　　　*The Tops.*

10. Avoid the "Thump-A-Bump" by Carving your Turns

For the majority of us, the best way to ski moguls is to slow down and make controlled carved turns though them. We suggest you spend a lot of time on easier mogul runs practicing your CPCPU, combined with extending and absorbing as you ski. One trick we share with aspiring mogul skiers is to look for a bump run that is short and running adjacent to a groomed run. That is the perfect place to practice the different mogul skiing techniques we have talked about in this section. Many ski areas now groom one side of the mogul run, so you can easily escape the bumps if you get tired or the terrain becomes too difficult. To introduce you to skiing the ruts, sides, or tops; try traversing into the mogul run near its end. With only four or five rows of moguls to contend with, your pucker factor goes way down, and you can concentrate on the job at hand. We recommend you ski one line repeatedly, until you feel comfortable skiing in the ruts, on the sides, and over the tops. Skiing the same line allows you to memorize it, and enables you to think more about practicing the different turn types. You stop worrying about what terrain change is coming next, because you already know it.

Mix it up and use all three styles to get through the bumps. If you are most comfortable skiing the ruts, do it until you reach the last row just before the run exits onto groomed terrain, and then throw in a turn off the side of the last bump. Next time, ski up to and over the top of the last bump. I am sure you know what I am going to say now; make another run trying these different turning techniques for two or three rows of bumps. This kind of practice will keep you from developing a "barely surviving" style of bump skiing where you are banging into the bumps in a constant mode of recovery. People banging down through the bumps can often be heard as well as seen. Watch as they drop from row to row slamming into one bump after another. Where is the beauty in that?

11. How to Safely Learn to Ski Bumps

Learning to ski bumps is an incremental process that leads to expert performance. With this in mind, know that you do not have to jump right into the gnarliest mogul field to develop your skills. The following list gives you some tips on how to safely and methodically approach mogul skiing.

1. Learn by practicing new techniques and movements while skiing slowly. Increasing your speed before improving your skills never works in the moguls.
2. Pick your battles carefully:
   a. Practice on shorter, moderately sloped mogul runs.
   b. Ski on soft, packed powder bumps whenever possible. Resist the urge to enter hard or icy moguls until your fundamentals are solidly developed.
   c. Before you ski, analyze the run in front of you. You may notice, for example, that the middle has the largest bumps and that on the left side, the snow is scraped off from too

much traffic, making the right side, in this case, the best for skiing. Ski it.

    d. Analyze the run for fall line options. You want to ski directly down the fall line in moguls, so be sure to look back and forth across the slope to see where the fall line looks the best. If possible, you want to avoid skiing down any part of the run that slopes off to one side or the other. For a detailed description of identifying the fall line look on pages 32 and 33. It is more difficult to ski moguls formed on a side-hill portion of the run.

    e. Now you are ready to choose your line through the bumps. After looking uphill for oncoming skiers, you can traverse across the run and look down various lines. One line may look nice for a few rows, but ends in a big wall. Another may be too deeply rutted and is to be avoided by the savvy bump skier. Usually, hiding among these bad lines will be one that's better, and appears to run for a greater distance down the hill. This is your line: Nail it!

    f. Don't practice only in the bumps. Your mogul skiing can benefit copiously from practicing short swing turns on the groomed runs. To review the section on short turns see pages 93 -98.

3. Use low angle runs with small moguls to practice one skill at a time. For example, practice the correct way of planting your poles for an entire run, then switch to concentrating on standing tall for a run. The next run can be your time to make the legs work in unison with the feet staying close together, and don't forget to take a run working on your hip projection, in which your legs absorb the bump and then extend down the back side.

Note: If being in the back seat is a habitual problem for you, try exaggerating your arm position by pushing your arms further out in front of you. Now this is something you definitely want to do on an easy mogul run because it will feel awkward at first. Push those arms out in front of you until your elbows are just slightly bent. Make a few runs concentrating only on this arm position. Now, go out and have fun in the bumps as you carve smooth turns down the fall line.

12. Does Equipment Make a Difference?

Yes. To effectively ski the bumps you want a boot that flexes more easily forward at the ankle than a race boot. You will also fair better if your skis are narrower at the waist than a freeride, big mountain, or powder ski. A narrower waist allows you to get the ski from edge to edge more quickly. It is best to stay away from race or carving skis, and look for a ski with a softer flex and good torsional rigidity.

Mogul Skier at Sqaw Valley, CA.

Visit our website for more self-help tools on Mogul Skiing: www.weekendwarriorsguide.com

DVD: A Weekend Warrior's Guide to Real Moguls, Expert Runs
E-Booklet: A Weekend Warrior's Guide to Mogul Skiing Technique

CHAPTER 16

CRUD SKIING

Skiing crud requires you to keep your feet together, distribute your weight more evenly between your skis, and add a bit of aggression. The most important component of crud skiing rests in your ability to vary the downward pressure you exert on your skis during a turn. The amount of force you transfer to your skis (the CP of CPCPU) is dependent on the thickness of the crust at the top of the cruddy snow, and the density of the snow underneath this top layer. If you can vary the amount of pressure quickly when turning in crud, you will stay on your feet. Push on your skis until they just break through the crud and then keep pushing until you force your skis to come around in the turn. Finish by rebounding up out of the snow to un-weight your skis. Exert too little pressure and you can not drive the skis into the crud and hold your line. Exert too much pressure and you break through too far and auger into the crud, unable to bounce out and make the next turn.

Almost no one skis the crud. I think it is a fear of the unknown, combined with that inalienable human desire to look great when skiing, that keeps most of us out of it. Struggling through the crud can quickly make you look bad, if not down right ugly. I can remember a particular day when I was standing above a steep and imposing section of cruddy snow, while one of my friends watched from below as I entered the run. It turned out to be a series of flying one footed linked turns complimented with flailing arms and hands. Luckily, I arrived at the bottom without falling and was rewarded with an appropriate comment from my partner. "Well, you made it through, but it wasn't pretty."

We should first try to define crud before we talk about how to ski it. Crud is typically a multilayer, breakable, crusty, or semi-frozen packed powder type of snow. It's not hard pack, powder, corduroy, ice, or slush. Most of the time, it is snow that has formed a degree of breakable crust on top of one or more layers of snow that has fallen in the past several weeks. Crud is formed in the aftermath of a storm when the snow is exposed to varying

137

temperatures, additional moisture, and wind. The varieties of crud are endless, and can vary from one to several layers deep, and even be hiding under a few inches or more of fresh light powder. It can be frustrating to ski if you don't have the skills needed to successfully negotiate through the nastiest of snow conditions.

For our purposes here we are going to focus on talking about crud that consists of breakable, layered crust formed on top of softer snow. Most other kinds of crud are just not worth skiing, especially if they are of the frozen variety. Skiing frozen crud brings little to no joy, even if you can do it like an expert. Most people just want to get off this rough, rock-hard surface and look for something more rewarding.

To be an effective crud skier you must be willing to dedicate time and effort to it. You need to be willing to fall numerous times, perhaps hundreds of times, and you must have a strong desire to conquer it. If you do master it, your ability to ski successfully all over the mountain will be greatly enhanced. There will be days when no one else wants to ski, but you will be out there skiing breakable crud and enjoying it as if it were new fallen powder.

The following tips and techniques will give you an understanding of how to survive and even enjoy your runs in the crud. Experts do it run after run and so can you.

Tips and Techniques for Crud Skiing

1. Keep your Feet Together.
2. Ski With your Skis More Evenly Weighted, as if on a Platform.
3. Apply the Basic Fundamentals of Skiing Technique.
4. Apply Graduated Pressure to your Skis in the Turns.
5. Use an Aggressive Style to Penetrate the Crust.
6. Practice, Practice, Practice, Practice.

1. Keep Your Feet Together

Attempting to ski crud with your feet separated by even as little as six inches is not a wise decision. This increases the likelihood that your skis will separate and go in opposite directions, making your legs feel like the wishbones of a Thanksgiving turkey. Result: you fall, lose a ski, and have a tough time standing up. Using simultaneous foot movements will not allow your skis to go in separate directions. Adding uniform legs movements and a dash of aggression will get you well on your way to successful crud skiing.

Figure 16.1 *Ski Crud with an Imaginary Belt around the Knees. The skier keeps the knees close together, not as if glued together like in powder skiing, but ranging from touching to several inches apart. Keeping the knees just slightly apart in crud helps maintain balance when applying pressure to the skis in the turn. Attack the turn with a flexed core.*

2. Ski with Your Skis More Evenly Weighted

You do not want to enter into crud using the "outside ski dominant" approach to weighting your skis. For crud, you should always distribute your weight more evenly across both skis. Our preferred weight distribution is D65 U35, as noted in the chart on page 103. You will want more weight on the outside ski to help you power through the initial crust, but you do need to have significant weight on the inside ski as well so it won't take off in the wrong direction. One trick I use in crud is to ***strongly flex my leg muscles and core*** (as contrasted to powder skiing) when pushing through the turn.

139

This gives me the ability to hold my legs together when being pushed around by the crud, and it supplies my skis with the necessary power to blast through the crud. Part two of this trick requires you to modulate this increased pressure as needed between the fronts and backs of your skis. For example, you can apply force to the tails of your skis by driving your ankles forward while pushing down on your heels. This maneuver drives the tips of your skis up to the surface. This only works if you stay centered fore and aft over your skis. Your romps through breakable or top crusted crud will go well if you consistently keep your tips visible right at the surface. In other crud conditions, your tips may sink a little, but will become visible at the end of the turn and through the transition phase between turns.

In crud, you come up out of the turn by rebounding off your skis in combination with jumping out of the crud. It should be sufficient to use flexing (rebounding) and extending; only add the jumping when the crud becomes difficult to break out of. These flexing and jumping actions become more explosive if the crust is thick and the snow underneath is dense. In the most difficult crud, you might need to jump completely out of the snow in order to turn.

3. Apply the Basic Fundamentals of Ski Technique

In the crud, utilizing the fundamentals of good upper body positioning as your lower body supplies energy to your skis, is more critical than in any other type of snow. Crud will bounce you around and grab at your skis without warning, causing them to separate and dive. Because the nature of crud skiing is so unpredictable, you need to be at the ready all the time, constantly responding to different feedback from the snow.

If your body is always correctly positioned, you will be able to adjust for variances in the crud as you successfully cut it up. The one really big secret is to keep those arms in the beach ball position, or to return them to it very quickly if you get out of position. This technique still requires that you do not panic during the rougher sections of your journey through the crud. When you get knocked out of position, ignore it and focus only on thrusting your arms back in front of you and up high where they belong. This will help save you. Yes, there will be times during which you may be out of balance and accelerating for a distance, but get those arms back in position and you can immediately initiate a turn to bring it all back under control again. If you feel your legs against the back of your boots, your arms are out of position, so thrust them forward.

At times the crud will have a single layer of breakable crust, and you will be unable to carve turns through it. To get through this type of snow you

140

rebound (explode) up out of the crud in order to initiate a turn. This technique is used in conditions that are just too difficult for a carved turn. To stay in control when doing this, you must land in the next turn centered over your skis with your arms held high and out in front of you. While in the air between turns use foot and leg steering to change directions. This explosive move is powerful and chunks of snow will be flying up as you tear through the crud, and that's cool

Figure 16.2 *In Severe Crud Explode Upward Out of the Turn: As your skis break free from the snow initiate the next turn using foot steering to quickly change directions. (See pages 94 and 95 for details on foot steering.)*

4. Apply Graduated Pressure to Your Skis in the Turns

Mastering dense snow or full blown breakable crud can only occur when you have learned to use the feedback you get from the snow while turning. We have discussed going straight into a series of turns so your first turn need be only a half turn, and that is also the case in crud. This half turn is easier to make, and offers a higher rate of success when you have no idea what the snow will be like. However, success in the crud is directly related to your ability to translate feedback coming up from your skis into usable action.

On your first turn, the crust may break easily and the snow underneath might be correspondingly light, then you know that only a moderate amount of pressure is necessary to make turns in this snow. On the other hand, if the crust is firm and the under layer is dense, you will need to apply more pressure to keep your skis on their line through the turn. This is a skill you learn with practice and it requires concentrating on how your skis push back at you during the turn. As you make more turns, you will get more information about the consistency of the snow, and soon you will know about how much pressure you should use through each turn.

THERE IS A CAVEAT HERE: Never assume that the amount of pressure needed to control your skis in the turn remains the same throughout the entire run, or even the entire turn. Typically you will enter into a turn pushing less on your skis than you do at the end of the turn. This is true most of the time, in every condition. Snow conditions change from the beginning of the run to the end, and the longer run, the more dramatic the change can be to the snow. This can require you to push with more or less force through your turns in one part of the run as compared with another part.

You will find that snow conditions also change within the same run if the run's angle to the sun changes. For example, conditions will change if the top of the run faces north, but the bottom half bends around the mountain taking on a south facing aspect. Since south faces get more sun in the winter (at least where we live) they will solidify sooner and won't be as much fun to ski as the north faces. When skiing crud and other conditions around the mountain, be aware of slope aspect (NSWE) and make a mental note reminding you where the good snow is that day. Many resorts have more than one mountain, and knowing which aspect has the good snow can be a big help in making your day more pleasurable. Did I just digress again, going from discussing crud to rambling somewhat about aspect? Oh well, it's all good.

5. Use an Aggressive Style to Penetrate Crusted-Over Crud

Frankly, being more aggressive works in any type of crud. By nature it is heavier, rougher, and more unpredictable than other types of snow. Just to clarify up front, we are saying be more aggressive in your movements, and we are not inferring that you should ski faster and crazier to be successful in the crud. Aggression in crud relates to using more leg muscle to push on your skis and to hold your skis in their turn line. It also applies to exiting turns in the crud, where you must jump up and elongate your entire body to free your skis from the muck below you.

When the crud is really bad, "jump rope" to escape and redirect your skis into the next turn. This turn is effective in double-layered crud, where you need to be careful not to break through the second tier of crusted snow. In this condition, rather than exploding off your skis, you need to up un-weight off the lower layer of crust after breaking through the surface. This allows you to turn without breaking through the lower layer in the crud. If you break through both layers it will be very difficult to stay on your feet. This is a more subtle turning technique than the rebound turn used to explode out of the snow. In the rebound turn you will use significant downward pressure on your skis to explode up out of the snow. When using the jump turn you up un-weight the instant you feel your skis contact the second layer in the crud. Again, this prevents you from breaking through the lower layer.

Figure 16.3 *Jump Rope to Break Out of the Crud. In difficult crud, exit the turn with an upward jumping or pulling up of the legs, but don't duck the head. Stand up and elongate the body.*

No one said skiing crud was relaxing and it isn't. Crud is not the medium for perfect turns, and you can feel really good about getting through it with no falls and a series of linked fall line turns.

6. Practice, Practice, Practice

Once upon a time there was a skier; not a crud skier, just a skier. But alas, this skier wanted to be a crud skier, and he was willing to do whatever it would take to be just that. It just so happened, this skier knew a really excellent crud skier, so he decided to ask this master of the crud, how to become an excellent crud skier himself.

The crud skier did not answer the question, and instead he just motioned to the lift. They both got on it and up they went to the very top of the mountain. Once there, they traversed further around the mountain than the skier had ever been. At last they arrived at a steep, out-of-the-way section of the mountain that just rolled down and disappeared, as if ending in a cliff.

Two weeks ago, it had snowed for nine straight days, and for the last five days the temperature had remained cold, but the wind blew every night. All this winter weather resulted in snow conditions that were less than ideal. In fact, this section of snow had about a three inch breakable crust on top of it, and that gave way to some relatively dense snow underneath, which in turn gave way to another layer of crust, and below that resided yet another layer of snow. All this added up to a double layer of crusted crud, and it was nearly un-skiable.

The crud skier still did not speak, and simply pushed straight off into this nastiest of snow. His first turn was only a half turn to the right and he broke through the top layer, but if you watched carefully you could see he knew just how much pressure to exert on his skis to ride on top of the second layer, while completing his next turn.

The novice crud skier said to himself; "that didn't look hard, so I think I'll try it," and he did. Instantly the results were different, as he made his first turn too big and without much momentum. He broke through the first layer, steadied himself for a second, and then broke right through the second layer, spinning around and falling upside down into the crud.

But, better times were ahead as on that day, this aspiring crud skier managed to make fourteen runs in this nastiest of snow. After six runs he had managed to link three turns without falling, and his excitement grew. Finally on the fourteenth run, he made it halfway without falling. He left the hill that day feeling he had learned the basics of crud skiing and knew he would be back for more.

IF YOU WANT TO SKI CRUD, UNLIKE THE 90% THAT NEVER VENTURE THERE, THEN YOU ALSO WILL NEED TO COME BACK FOR MORE PRACTICE, PRACTICE, PRACTICE.

CHAPTER 17

TREES – ARE NINETY PERCENT AIR

Trees are ninety percent air, but the other ten percent is so unforgiving that many ski related deaths occur when people hit them. Don't count on a helmet to save you. The force is that great. So, as we talk about tree skiing, remember the number one priority in the trees is your safety. In addition to worrying about hitting a tree, there is also the concern of falling into a well (or hole) created by the snow (actually the lack of it) around the base of a tree. Many people fall into tree wells and a certain number do not survive due to suffocation. Yes, you can suffocate in a tree well, where you might contribute to your own demise by attempting to dig your way out as the snow caves in on you.

Tree skiing can be a very fun and relatively safe activity if you just follow a few simple rules:

1) **Never ski alone in the trees, period.**
2) **Never lose sight of your companions.**
3) **Always wear a helmet and goggles. We wear helmets and goggles for all types of skiing, because it is safer and your goggles never fog when you put them on your helmet.**
4) **Know how to make kick turns, and be able to put your skis back on in deep powder before you go. There are no groomed runs in the trees.**

Skiing trees isn't about the trees themselves, it is about the white open space around and in between them. This is your target, your focus, and your place to be when skiing in the trees. It is this white space that will provide you with a skiing adventure that, unto itself, is totally fulfilling.

The trees seem to tighten together as often as they seem to open up and give way to the white space between them. The amazing thing about this opening and closing is that there almost always is a way to ski through it. Well, that last statement is mostly true after you have been skiing trees for a long time. Why? The experienced tree skier knows a few tricks of the trade that helps guide them through the random pattern of open space created by trees.

But, before we talk about these tricks of the trade, you should know that tree skiing is an advanced type of skiing. It is necessary for you to have mastered all the techniques covered up to this point, including crud skiing.

Tree skiing is sure to take you through every type of snow condition. Expect it.

Now let's talk tricks. First, you need to learn how to see the big picture and not focus only on the trees blocking your path. Look around and beyond the trees, scouting ahead for a continuing route through them. Always keep the trees somewhere in your vision, but bring the white space into sharp focus and find your line. If you are skiing into an ever tightening group of trees, glance left and right for an escape route and take the first one that opens up. As you make this jog continue to look left, right, and ahead through the trees for the next big open space (glade) as you continuously plan your descent. This is big picture vision.

Figure 17.1 *The Line Skied Through the Trees is Seldom Straight Down.*
Continually look right and left for traverses that will connect the open white spaces.

146

The next great tree skiing trick involves speed management: Too slow and your skis bog down, and too fast is dangerous. So, what does that leave us? In my world what's left is just right. The big question is what speed is correct for tree skiing. The answer is just a little faster than too slow. You need to be able to carry the speed necessary to float your skis in powder and break through the crud. The concern here is that speeds that are only moderate for a groomed slope, seem much faster in the confined arena of the trees. These speeds belong only in the realm of the advanced tree skier, and are not to be taken lightly. We strongly suggest you learn to ski trees with a trusted friend or ski instructor that can safely guide you through the experience.

Part of this experience will sometimes include skiing into tightly spaced trees, from which there is no escape route. Your trick here is to slam on the brakes by throwing down one big hockey stop. Be aware this could happen at any time, and you will need to stop instantly with your feet out in front of you, not your head. You can best accomplish this by literally yanking your skis out of the snow and jamming them back into the snow going across the fall line (the traverse direction). You will need to whip those skis sideways and stomp on them as you throw your upper body into the snow on the uphill side. Why throw your body uphill? Because in deep snow it is very easy to high side, and fly down the hill head first into a tree. An example of high siding is when a motorcycle rider brakes suddenly, causing the back wheel to slide sideways. During this slide, if the rear of the bike suddenly stops sliding, it creates tremendous force, ejecting the rider over the top of the motorcycle and out in front of it. The same thing happens if you are standing tall at the precise moment the skis are pushed deep into the snow at a sideways angle. This causes your body weight to shift toward the downhill side of your skis, and the resulting force ejects you out over your skis, and down toward the trees.

Finally, following an expert through the trees is a great trick you can use for learning how to correctly shred the foliage. Most people are eager to share their expertise with you, and they will likely take it easy on you for a few runs. This is actually a two part trick, and the second half is the part where you don't follow the expert. What I mean is you don't ski exactly in his tracks. Hopefully, this expert takes you into the not-so-tight trees the first few times, and there will be plenty of room to mimic his tracks. You can do this by skiing right next to the line he has laid down through the greenery. This allows you to experience untracked snow, and it keeps your speed down. I am sure you know that skiing in someone else's track always speeds you up.

Our summary thoughts on skiing the trees are the following:

1. Use big picture vision to plan several turns ahead of you.
2. Great tree skiers rarely touch any branches. A branch larger than ½ inch in diameter is going to knock you off your feet.
3. Skiing trees is a proactive endeavor. Make smooth and controlled turns, always feeling the changing snow under your feet, and adjusting your turn pressure accordingly.
4. Make traverses left or right in the trees to find a new open space to ski.
5. Focus on the open white space, and not on the trees. But never let the trees leave your vision.
6. Wear a helmet, and know how to kick turn, side step, and traverse in deep or cruddy snow.
7. Practice putting your skis on in deep powder, while standing near a groomed run.
8. Don't forget your goggles; they are your best defense against an eye injury that may be caused by connecting with a sharp branch.
9. Never ski the trees in early season. Not all the trees are upright in the forest, and it takes a lot of snow to cover the downed ones. If your ski dives under a log it will hurt a lot. Avoid skiing through any bumps or mounds of snow you see.
10. Never ski in the trees alone. Duh, I didn't need to say that.
11. Never ski fast or out of control in the trees.
12. Just like in the powder, fat skis work well in the trees.
13. Skiing the trees is taking a calculated risk. Be very careful!

CHAPTER 18

THE STEEPS

40, 50, or 60 degrees; how steep is steep? Snow starts to look steep at about twenty eight degrees, and this is especially true in confined or narrow ski terrain. You probably remember all the buzz about how incredibly steep the start was to the men's downhill in the 2002 Olympics at Snow Basin, Utah. It measured in at 45 degrees for the first 400 vertical feet, after which racers were already approaching seventy miles per hour according to reporters on the scene.

I think this validates that when you ski the steeps, gravity makes its incredible force known very quickly. If you were to point your skis straight down a 45-degree slope for just one second you would soon become a believer, as you experienced the phenomenal acceleration. It is this propensity toward acceleration that you need to control to effectively ski the steeps. But, that is not all you need to control on the steeps: Your fear must also be managed and kept down to a level that is healthy, but not distracting.

In this section we will be dealing with the techniques, strategies, and tactics you will need to ski the steeps while keeping your speed under control, and your fear at bay. The information in this chapter is directed at skiing only inside area boundaries. With rare exception, most ski areas in the United States do not have slopes of significant length that exceed a 40-degree pitch. The majority of lengthy, steep slopes (45 to 60-degrees) are located in the backcountry, and those are a subject for another day.

Yet, just because we are focusing on slopes of 28 to 40-degree angles, does not make them any less intimidating. When the snow is hard and slick, there is no difference between a fall on a on 35-degree or a 45-degree slope. Either one will act like a giant, slippery slide with gravity pulling you toward the bottom at an amazing rate of speed. Skiing firm, steep snow is scary on your best day, and your fear of falling here, with the resulting pain and possible injury, is exactly what keeps you from skiing it well.

If you are like us, while riding the chairlift at any magnificent high mountain resort, you may occasionally daydream about what an adventure it would be to take the high traverse to the mouth of those distant chutes and rock strewn faces. Once there, you dream of making a flawless descent back down to where the average skiers languish the day away on the groomed runs. Hopefully, we can help you with your dream, but first you will need one good tool (literally), and a few tricks to get ready to ski the steeps.

On the steeps, staying in complete control is the hallmark of an expert skier, and it is this discipline that keeps them alive. When slopes approach 35 degrees or steeper, a fall can result in significant injury or death. It is for this reason that skiing the steeps takes high level skills and a healthy respect for your own mortality.

Sergio in the Italian Alps: Hey Serg, I can't see a way out from here.

In the winter of 2006 we were skiing in Alagna, a ski area referred to as the LaGrave of Italy. Alagna is currently gaining world-wide recognition as a ski area offering extreme ski terrain, and while I was there, I had the chance to descend a few of their chutes and cliff faces that make up the fabric of this developing reputation. I approached these extreme steeps with respect, as falling on some of this terrain meant certain death.

Accompanied by an Italian guide named Sergio, I enjoyed exciting descents down chutes with slope angles north of 50 degrees. One of these was only 184 centimeters wide at the top. I know this because that was the exact length of the skis attached to my boots. To descend this chute we side-stepped down the firm snow to a small ramp where we could make a kick turn, followed by another side-stepping sequence that took us over a three meter section of ice. Once below this we were able to link turns, as the narrow chute widened.

On this day I was a bit more nervous than is usual for me. My apprehension stemmed from being without my self-arrest (SA) grips, which are always my primary defense against fear when skiing the steeps. This grip functions like an ice axe as you thrust it into the snow to keep you from sliding off steep faces into the abyss below. I did not have these special grips on this day because none were available in this region of the Alps. Not having them put my senses on high alert the entire day, and I skied with more reserve than would be normal for me.

The first self-arrest grip I saw was developed more than two decades ago by a ski equipment icon named Paul Ramer. It is pictured in Figure 18.1 on the right, and although today's modern versions vary, the principle remains the same. There is some sort of blade attached to the grip of your ski pole, and when you fall, the blade is thrust into the snow and dragged down the slope, biting into the surface until you come to a stop. Without self-arrest grips, in many steep situations, you will fall and slide until you hit immovable objects (usually rocks) or until you reach the bottom of the slope. Long falls on steep terrain most often result in minor to severe injury or death.

These bladed grips can save lives and reduce injury, but you should never depend on them as a guarantee you won't get hurt when skiing steep slopes. The grips allow you to relax more, and concentrate on the task at hand instead of being engulfed in fear.

It is this notion of self-arrest grips alleviating fear that brings me back to my Alps story again.

Figure 18.1 *Self-Arrest Grips. When the going gets tough you can't live without them! Many steep descents in the USA and Europe carry with them the moniker "If you fall, you die." But, not with grips this arresting.*

During the trip, a few of us hired a guide and boarded a helicopter bound for a high plateau at 14,500 feet above sea level in the Alps. Our goal was to ski down the glaciers to the village, about 8500 vertical feet below us. Everyone was having a good time until we came upon a narrow constriction filled with a few meters of ice. Below it skiing looked good again, and we decided to side-step down this few feet of ice with our skis on. It seemed unnecessary to rope up for safety. However, this icy section was about 45-degrees steep, so the guide went first as a confidence builder for the rest of us. Just after him a second skier started to descend, wanting the guide to stay close below and offer moral support. Then it happened; the second skier started to get anxious and slipped on the ice, falling into the guide. They slid together for a short distance before the guide was able to stop. The anxious skier was not so lucky, and plummeted 1500 vertical feet to the valley floor. This person received cuts and bruises, was knocked unconscious, and suffered some abrasions, but lived through the fall to ski another day. In the Alps, a fall of that distance almost always ends in death, but amazingly this skier was launched off a snow ramp and flew over many meters of rock debris before landing safely on the other side in the snow. Self-arrest grips probably would have given this skier the confidence to side step down the short icy section, knowing a fall would only result in a few feet of sliding, as compared to a 1500 vertical foot screamer.

These special grips are not just a tool for the backcountry, and can be very useful inside ski area boundaries as well. I have personally witnessed serious falls on black diamond and double black diamond runs that resulted in people sliding from 500 to 1000 vertical feet, and sustaining injuries that would have been avoided if they were able to arrest their slide with this type of grip. When using these grips, be aware that you can injure yourself on the blades, so it is imperative you practice using them before it gets serious. If you are going to practice stopping yourself with these grips, be sure to practice on a slope that loses its steepness in a very short distance and has a safe run out at the bottom; devoid of rocks, trees, and obstacles in general. It is also a good idea to have someone with experience using the grips, show you how to use them. These grips will never be a substitute for good ski technique, but they do add a margin of safety.

Skiing the steeps is an adventure, but I am *not encouraging* you to go looking for steep skiing, with or without these special grips. You need to decide for yourself when it is your time to go in search of this scarier and more dangerous type of skiing. To help prepare you, we want to talk about the following:

1. An On-Snow Drill that Prepares You for the Steeps.
2. Make Sure your Equipment is Ready.
3. Precise, Solid, and Progressive Edge Sets.
4. The Importance of Body Position.
5. Specialty Turns for Special Situations.
6. Turn like a European Ski Guide.

1. On-Snow Drill that Prepares You for the Steeps

On steep slopes, lingering in the fall line between turns leads to quick acceleration and a loss of control for the average skier. The secret is to keep your skis out of the fall line by making very short turns, bringing your skis back and forth across the fall line quickly. This requires you to keep your upper body quiet and facing down the fall line, with your feet and skis carving below you. Yes I said carving, as opposed to pivoting or jumping. Hopping, pivoting, and jumping are special turn techniques that need only be employed in select situations. Use these special turn techniques when skiing very steep slopes in extreme crud, powder, slush, and confined spaces.

Carving your turns on the steeps gives you the highest degree of control, and is achievable by the average advanced skier on up to 40 degree slope angles. Expert steep skiers can carve their turns at even higher angles. The question is: How do you learn to do this? The answer is you practice it in a safe environment. This entire book has been pinpointed at learning to carve turns by keeping pressure on your skis and keeping them on edge through the turn. This remains true as we help prepare you to ski the steeps.

On-Snow Steep Skiing Drill

1. Pick a groomed intermediate run with a moderate slope angle.
2. Repeatedly make a series of short turns, staying directly in the fall line. Keep these turns confined to a narrow corridor as you descend.
3. Once comfortable with step 2, take it to a steeper groomed slope.
4. Again, make sets of short turns directly down the fall line.
5. Be sure to ski the steeper run at the **same speed** as the intermediate run.
6. Now, ski these steeper runs making short turns, and descend as slowly as possible.
7. It may help to practice linked hockey stops in the fall line, applying only enough pressure to stay stable in the turn. Don't be too aggressive, be precise and apply just enough edge pressure to complete the turn. Practice this repeatedly.

TIP: You know you have mastered this drill when you can descend a steep groomed slope at a very slow pace, while linking short turns down a narrow corridor *not wider than ten feet*. Do this drill moving as slowly as possible on the steepest groomed run you can find at your local area.

Over the course of three decades I have practiced this drill thousands of times. I now automatically do it for a short distance every time I come upon a steep section on a groomed run. You will not be successful on the steeps if you wait until you are looking down a 40 degree slope to practice.

2. Make Sure your Equipment is Ready

When skiing the steeps, you can find yourself in situations that put heavy demands on your equipment. This is just the nature of steep skiing as it is often found in cliff areas, near or in chutes, and down mixed media slopes. Mixed media slopes are typically some combination of trees, glacial boulders, cliff bands, and varying fall line angles. Therefore, it makes good sense to have your equipment in top operating condition.

You should tune your skis prior to any steep skiing for a variety of reasons. You will need sharp edges and flat ski bases to facilitate finessing your edge sets, and for making sure your edges release and grab correctly in response to your lower body input. Your boots and bindings need to be ramped appropriately in relation to your body characteristics, so you will stand centered fore and aft over your skis. This helps you initiate your turns from the correct position, and ensures you can make quick turns without struggling. Your boots must fit snugly, and be correctly aligned to your body type before you enter the steeps. For details on alignment and boot fit see chapters 23 and 24.

Because force placed on your equipment can be greater in steep terrain, it is also important to make sure your bindings are properly adjusted. Never depend on someone else to choose your settings. Be honest with yourself when increasing or decreasing your binding settings, and use the recommended DIN settings for your weight, age, and skill level as a starting point. From there you may find it necessary to increase your binding settings in order to hold you on challenging and steep terrain. If you choose to make adjustments, approach it with extreme caution, and do only small changes each time. You need to decide what settings work best for you to avoid premature release when skiing difficult and steep terrain. It is prudent to seek out the advice of equipment professionals before making any adjustments to your bindings.

3. Precise, Solid, and Progressive Edge Sets

Skiing the steeps is about making an edge set and then transitioning quickly to the next solid edge set placed in exactly the right place. During the edge set, it is critical that you apply just the right amount of force in the right way. If you panic and jump on your edges trying to stop your momentum, as in a radical hockey stop, you can slide or skid. This generally results in a loss of control, and the skid can turn into a full fledged fall.

Typically, aspiring steep skiers let their mind dictate body position, and they often shy away from the downhill side of their skis and lean up hill. It's the fear factor the causes this to happen, and they do this because it feels more secure to lean back up the hill. This is a big mistake because when you tilt uphill it releases the force on your edges and they blow out from under you.

Figure 18.2 *Upper Body Faces Downhill Over the Skis, Keeping Pressure on the Edges. The skier on the left has lost control of the ski edges, and is sliding downward. Leaning into the hill, and rotating the upper body out of the fall line causes this type of fall. The skier on the right has moved the hips toward the uphill direction, while the upper body is facing downhill into the fall line. The upper body, above the hips, is tipped slightly downhill as well, helping to keep pressure on the ski edges. When skiing the steeps, use a series of short turns, because there is not time to rotate the body in and out of the fall line.*

To keep from losing edge grip, you need to load your skis with an elastic leg. Keeping your legs buoyant enables you to progressively weight your skis as needed. This concept is best thought of as using your legs like progressive rate shock absorbers that can apply variable force on the edges, and just as quickly release it. It is really just the up and down movements of a carved turn done at a faster pace with more attention to changes needed in edge pressure – not too much, and not too little. It takes practice to learn how to modulate or finesse your edges on steep terrain to get just the right amount of grip. Here on the steeps, your turns need to be quick and round, with minimal or no time spent pointing your skis straight down the fall line. To assist your edges in the turn, you will also need to do certain movements with your upper body.

4. The Importance of Body Position

To enhance your edge sets on the steeps you will need to use the hip slide technique. If you slide your hips in the uphill direction, while rotating your upper body into the fall line, it will create counter-rotation and hip angulation at the same time. Trust me, it just happens, so don't worry about understanding either counter-rotation or hip angulation. Just do the following exercise.

156

DURING THIS EXERCISE YOU ARE DOING THREE MOVEMENTS AT ONE TIME:

(1) FLEXING YOUR ANKLES FORWARD, (2) ROTATING THE UPPER BODY INTO THE FALL LINE, (3) AND SLIDING YOUR HIPS UPHILL.

REMEMBER TO KEEP YOUR ARMS IN THE BEACH BALL POSITION.

Secret Tip: Move through this exercise very slowly until you feel a significant increase of pressure on the uphill edge of your downhill ski.

Isn't that great fun? All you need to do is stand on the hill and look silly to completely understand hip rotation and hip angulation. If want to look even goofier, point to the angle created by your upper and lower body and bring your hand across the front of your waist showing your audience that your hips are slightly rotated in a direction different from your skis. So what's the point of this exercise?

The point is to get you ready to ski the steeps with you in control of the terrain, instead of the other way around. You know it is all coming together when your hips are facing almost directly downhill as you set your edges with your skis facing across the run. At the moment of edge set, you should be planting your pole firmly in front of you just below your boots. This pole plant position is necessary to facilitate quick short turns.

Figure 18.3 *Aggressive Edge Engagements. 1. With the ankles driven forward, turn the hips (face them downhill) into the fall line. 2. Simultaneously slide the hips uphill. 3. During the hip slide, make sure the upper body remains out over the skis, and does not lean back up the hill. This is the correct position at the time of edge set, and the skis are loaded with energy. Rebound up and turn from this position*

By now you are well aware of what happens next. This strong edge set and pole plant give way to a release of stored energy. You use this energy to rebound up and around into the next turn. If feels great to allow your upper body to actually lead your lower body into the turn. For just a second, it feels like your feet forgot to follow along. This feeling is created by your body's center of mass crossing over your skis into the next turn. In the steeps, the transfer of your body mass back and forth across your skis occurs more up and down the fall line, as opposed to side-to-side when carving on the groomers. On the steeps up to 45-degrees, except in chutes or other confined turning areas, continue to use the CPCPU carving technique. We carve our turns everywhere on the "moderate" steeps unless a specialty turn is called for, to get us through a difficult situation. The only change is in your pole plant placement. You now plant on your downhill side near your boot, instead of at the tip of your ski.

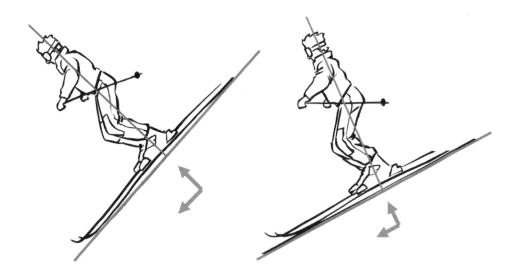

Figure 18.4 *A Skier's Body Always Remains Perpendicular to the Slope. The steeper it gets, the further forward or outward you must lean. It helps to push your arms out further in front of you to make your upper body lean out in the downhill direction. The skier on the left is on a 50-degree slope, and the skier on the right is on a 25-degree slope. On steep terrain, this perpendicular position occurs for only a nanosecond in the fall line, as the skier transitions from one turn to the next. Never lean back as it gets steeper.*

5. Specialty Turns for Special Situations

There are three unique types of turns you can use for special circumstances or conditions when skiing the steeps. They are the pedal turn, the hip check turn, and the kick turn. We use each of these turns in specific situations where a carved short-swing turn just won't work safely. Although it is beyond the scope of this book to discuss these turns in detail (which mostly have applications in the backcountry), we do want to share the basics of each with you.

First there is the ***pedal turn***, and we commonly use it when the conditions are horrid. It works great on the steepest slopes. Here you will find yourself in a position called *short leg, long leg.* Because it is so steep, your downhill leg is almost fully extended, and your uphill leg is sharply bent. Your feet are far apart, but your legs are close together and your uphill hand will be almost touching the snow. Yes, it's that steep. From this position you become an antigravity machine, and jump up by springing off your *uphill bent leg.*

This vertical up motion allows you to get both skis in the air and guide them around into the next turn. You literally swing both skis through the air and land on your edges facing the other direction. The term pedal comes from the image created as you push off your uphill bent leg, just like a bicyclist pushes on their bend leg to power the bicycle forward.

The ***hip check turn*** was made famous by extreme skier Scott Schmidt. He used it as a control measure to slow down in challenging terrain, and the basic principle of the turn was to scrub speed by dragging your hip (the one on the inside of the turn) through the snow to provide additional friction. During this turn you do not sit down in the snow, as most of your weight is still being forced onto your skis. Watch a DVD on this, or have someone demonstrate it before you try it. From our perspective, it is a soft-snow-only maneuver.

That brings us to the ***kick turn***. This is a specialty turn that you can use repeatedly when skiing in tight situations such as chutes, or among cliff bands. It is my favorite escape turn when you just can't make any other type of turn. *It is performed from a complete stop.* You may already be familiar with the kick turn, and able to do it. But, doing it on moderate slopes is quite different from doing it on the steeps.

To benefit from it on the steeps, you need to be able to perform the turn in limited space and without moving down or across the hill more than a tiny bit. This turn is scary when performed on the steep slopes, because you will have your skis pointing in opposite directions at the midpoint of the move. It starts with your skis facing across the hill. The goal is to lift the downhill ski up and flop it over so that it is pointing in the opposite direction of your uphill ski. Next, you simply lift your uphill ski up and flop it over, placing it along side your other ski. When you have completed the turn, you should be facing 180 degrees from where you started.

160

Figure 18.5. *Learning a Kick Turn on a Steep Slope.* One person stands above, and firmly grasps the bottom of the lower skier's jacket to prevent him from falling forward during the kick turn. The lower skier then picks up the downhill ski and flops it over, placing it on the snow. Now it is facing the opposite direction of his uphill ski. Next, the lower skier picks up his uphill ski and rotates it around next to the other ski. Both skis are now pointing a new direction. As the second ski is rotated, move the uphill pole to the downhill side and plant it for balance as the move is finished.

Before doing this exercise, be sure you are flexible enough to attempt it without injury. Be careful not to hit your assistant with your skis or poles as you rotate them into the new direction. The skier grasping your jacket must have their skis facing across the hill in the direction your skis will be pointing *after the kick turn has been completed (fig. 18.5).* In other words, the exercise starts out with one skier facing right and one skier facing left.

6. Turn like a European Ski Guide

We have skied with many guides from the Alps, and one thing is very evident about their skiing. They carve their turns everywhere they go. We have skied with them on a variety of terrain, in various conditions, and the turn remains the same. To us, the typical turn made by a European guide is the epitome of the classic carved turn. Each turn forms a perfect half circle, with the skis always on edge.

The European guides make these turns appear easy and graceful, and they just look better than the other skiers on the mountain. Their skiing utilizes the time tested method of keeping pressure on the ski, putting it on edge, and letting it make the perfect arc it was designed for. They always ski in control, and with a rhythm that flows equally in both directions.

The fun is in the search for the perfectly carved turn. With practice you can achieve "the arc." All it really takes is practicing the fundamentals over and over again. Practice frequently on the groomers, and soon you will be able to ski the steeps with style. CPCPU it.

Never ski fast on the steeps.
Control is your ally.

TIPS FROM THE EXPERTS

This is definitely going to be one of the shortest chapters in the book, but its value is significant *if you believe.* What you need to believe is that each of the following tips is worth a mountain of gold in the ski world. For the most part they are simple and to the point. If you implement each tip without questioning the validity, it will be the shortest path to improving your skiing technique. I believe what these experts have to say, and my skiing is fundamentally better today than it was twenty years ago.

As you read the tips you may hear a familiar ring, discovering that their advice sounds similar to much of the information put forth in this book. However, the interesting point is that none of these experts had read the book prior to offering their tip.

These tips come from a group of skiers that are masters in their chosen area. They are instructors, competitors, coaches, and champions. Believe them, and you will shorten your learning curve.

1. When skiing the glades, focus your attention on the gaps between the trees, not the trees you're skiing around and between. By concentrating on the open areas, you look ahead and find the clean line through the maze. Eyes lead our bodies, and where they go, we follow.
Stuart Andrews, coach and freestyle competitor

2. Mogul fields are a series of large troughs and bumps. Too often the skier looks for a path or line that consists of going from one trough or "hole" to the next. Next time, think of looking for the surface area of the mogul that gives you the smoothest place to complete a quick short turn. It can be on the front side, or back of the bump; and is often the opposite of the trough. Each turn is different so it will take a lot of practice applying the correct amount of pressure to the skis for each turn on each surface. By doing this you can direct your skis and control where you turn. So next time look down the hill and stay out of the holes!
Bill Campbell, American Pro Skiing Grand Prix Champion

3. Believe it: Everyone has bad days, and to break out of a bad day go back to the basics. Tell yourself to reach for the tip of your ski or the top of the mogul by flicking your pole plant to start or initiate your turn, and apply more pressure to the downhill ski.

Joey Cordeau, world mogul champion

4. If Robert Frost were alive today, he might advise skiers to choose the line less traveled, especially on powder days. Even at Steamboat Springs, one of the premier powder/tree skiing areas in the world with an abundance of expert skiers and riders, I'm amazed how much untracked snow can be found by being a little creative. For example, if you choose a line that is at a somewhat different angle to the obvious one that most people take, instead of constantly turning through the tracks of other skiers and riders, you barely notice their tracks as you cross them once and forget them. I've always chosen the line less skied, and it has made all the difference.

Todd Kelly, ski instructor

5. Don't be lazy with your hands. Although it may seem unnatural to continuously hold your hands high and in front of you (roughly chest level), it will allow you to keep a quiet upper body while maintaining a forward and balanced position during the turn. If your hands are in this position and your arms are relaxed with a slight bend; you are now in the driver's seat. Grab the steering wheel with elbows out and your palms facing each other, and ski great!

Mark Kraley, ski instructor

6. Most people are locked up below the fall line; never learning to ski both above and below it in a single turn. Whether you are accelerating or decelerating, you need to learn to do it above the fall line. To do this, you make the first half of your turn skiing into the fall line and the second half of your turn skiing away from the fall line. You must learn to put pressure on the new carving edge above the fall line, and carry it all the way through the complete turn. When you do this correctly it will result in a round carved turn, with you dictating your speed and rhythm.
(Authors' note: This is probably the single most important point made about carving turns, but because it is a difficult concept to grasp please see chapter 12 pages 88-90 for a complete explanation of skiing above and below the fall line.)

Dan Kurdy, racer, mogul competitor, film star

7. When asked by the author to contribute a skiing tip for this book, different ideas came to mind. Should I talk about keeping your hands up, ankle and knee flex, angulation, or staying centered on your skis? Then it came to me. None of it is going to help you if you're not physically strong enough to execute the drills or skiing techniques taught in these pages. I'm not trying to say you need to become a gym rat, but you need to be in decent shape. Skiing is a power sport and runs don't last that long.

You need to be explosive in order to hit the moguls hard and not be knocked down, throw your skis out to the side and make a turn, or to set a hard edge to get over a patch of ice. You must be enough of an athlete to control your body as well as your equipment. So, by all means read and learn from this book. Just get off the couch and get yourself in skiing condition before you hit the mountain. It will make your skiing experience more rewarding and more importantly help prevent injury.

John Zuck, freestyle team director, mogul competitor

The Other Tools

CHAPTER 20

GOAL SETTING AND MOTIVATION

GOAL SETTING: If structured correctly, goal setting becomes a powerful tool you can use in your quest to become an expert skier. Use our simple five step goal setting process and your skiing will improve.

MOTIVATION: Motivation is not created from external influences. It comes from within; emerging from your desire to achieve a goal and your belief that you can do it. The foundation of motivation is based on setting realistic goals, and then putting a process in place to achieve them.

Our intent here is not to give you a lengthy dissertation on becoming self-motivated. However, we will share with you the basic elements of goal setting and motivation. To set the stage a few observations are appropriate.

If the mile run was never measured for time elapsed, no one would be running it under four minutes. A motivated human being will always respond to measurement by improving. For example, when running a mile, improvement will occur even if the individual does nothing different, other than trying to beat the previously recorded time. This will happen, to a point, without changing any variables such as running shoes, diet, and breathing habits.

To accelerate the rate of improvement and take it to a higher level, you need to apply some detailed strategies around your goals. A good goal to set would be increasing the number of days you will ski next year, for this will certainly improve your skiing a little if you do nothing else differently. But, let's suppose you surround this basic goal with a little more detail, using our five steps. We will use the "increasing the number of days you will ski next year" goal to illustrate this concept of adding detail to your goal.

Step One: Set the goal. *I will ski more days next year.*

Step Two: Make the goal specific. *I will ski 10 more days next year.*

Step Three: The goal must be dynamic. *I will ski 10 more days next year, and going only several hours will count as a day.*

Step Four: Add a specific strategy to the goal. *Each time I go skiing I will practice one or two on-snow drills from the Weekend Warrior's Guide to Expert Skiing.*

Step Five: All goals must be written, printed out, and posted in plain site. You should type up your goal exactly as you want it to happen and post it in three places where you will see it every day for the entire season. *I will ski 10 more days next year by February 20th, and improve my carved turns and powder skiing.*

Writing your goals out is the single most important thing you can do to make them a reality. Be careful with this process, because writing down goals greatly increases you chance of making them come true. The point is; you will be achieving what you write down so script it carefully. I once crafted a goal geared toward obtaining a cabin in the mountains, surrounded by pine trees. I reached that goal, only to discover it was not exactly what I had in mind. This happened because I was not specific enough when making the goal, and instead the cabin ended up made of 2 x 8 boards on a busy highway several miles from the forest, with only a view of the mountains. Events like this have taught me to be more specific about the goals I write. My goal should have been more detailed and included specifics about location, foliage, privacy and type of construction.

Setting realistic and detailed goals creates the motivation within you to achieve your dreams. There are a few additional things you should think about when setting your goals. Set up your goals with short-term, intermediate, and long-term targets. This gives you stepping stones to your ultimate goal, and makes it seem less monumental in scope. Ask yourself if the goal is acceptable for you. Are you happy with your goal, or does it seem too easy or too difficult? Goals must always be measurable and they must target something meaningful to you.

A well-crafted goal is positive in nature, and makes you feel good when you visualize your future success. Think about the stepping stones you have created and imagine how you will feel as you reach each one. If the feeling isn't good, you should make slight adjustments that will allow you to feel better about the journey. Remember that the process is a dynamic one, and positive adjustments to your goals keep your motivation alive.

You can stay self-motivated by using a few techniques to stay on course for the long-term. Start by setting interval targets for your goals. An example for our "Ski More Days Next Year" goal might be to add one more day per month. After you have developed short-term targets, visualize the desired outcome and how it makes you feel. Hopefully the feeling will be good, and spur you on to reaching your milestone – the goal itself. Read your goals everyday as a reminder of where you are going.

I have a system for reading my goals daily that makes it simple, and only requires a moment of my time. I create abbreviations or codes that spell out my goal in a condensed form. I typed these codes on a small piece of paper and laminate it. Then I place several in strategic locations where I can easily access and read them. One of my favorite places is in my car where I will see it and read it every time I get in the car. Another is on the refrigerator, and because it is in code, I am the only one that can read it and it stays private.

A goal must always be a bit of a stretch for you. It should never be easy, but it should also never be unattainable.

GOAL SETTING WORKS!

VVV & C: DIRECTING THE SKIER INSIDE YOU

When I think back to my early days of skiing, I see myself like a bouncing ball. On the easier runs I would make a good turn or two and then a series of mediocre turns. I struggled to get in rhythm, and like the ball, I just seemed to endlessly go up and down in the quality of my turns. Even worse, if I ventured off the groomed runs I would totally tense up and just try to survive. To overcome this, I vowed to fight back against the mountain and keep trying harder until I could force every turn to be a great one. This approach didn't work because I was guiding myself with all the wrong cues. These cues (commands) were only about demanding that I go out there and ski great. I used anger, aggression, too much thinking, and a lot of tense muscle movement. I was trying to force success on myself without a well thought out plan.

What I lacked was a structured and simple mental approach to self improvement. I did not take the time to clearly understand the nuances of ski technique, and I was unwilling to practice on easier slopes to master the subtleties of skiing like an expert. I was not willing to give in to the "relaxed me" and purge my mind of all the negative thoughts. Further, I always put the burden entirely on me, and I was unwilling to seek out expert skiers for help.

I, like many of you, was a big jumble of nerves, had a restrictive self-image, and a negative attitude toward my skiing. How could it be that I always had at least one thing wrong with my ski experience on any given day? Why did I think I had brought the wrong skis to the hill, or that the snow wasn't quite right for me, or that I just couldn't get in the groove that day? Tomorrow was always going to be better, and when tomorrow came I would be excited about my chances for a great day, but somehow it was never as good as I had expected.

After years of this torture, for which I was willing to pay a considerable sum of money, I finally decided to do something about it. I got a plan. I talked to a lot of people to get ideas for my plan, and it finally evolved into a four step process for improvement. I even gave the plan a name. I called it the **VVV & C.** The three V's stand for View, Visualize, and Video, and the C is for Cleanse.

This plan took me from the farm in Montana to being a paid professional skier. How well the plan worked was a great surprise to me, and over the years I have talked with many other expert skiers who use a similar approach to self-improvement on skis. Your path to improvement starts with the first V. **Viewing** creates a good understanding of what it looks like to correctly carve turns. View as many instructional DVDs/videos as you can get your hands on. Your local ski shop may loan or rent them to you, and there are many available on the internet. I am not talking about the exciting ski adventure videos that consist mainly of cliff jumping, powder skiing, and rail riding. I am talking about instructional videos that primarily deal with how to carve turns in different types of snow.

Plan to watch these videos when you can commit your full attention to them. I mean really stare at the expert skiers, totally immersed in watching their actions. You will know your concentration level is at a maximum if you feel wide-eyed, open mouthed, and on the verge of drooling. The thought of looking this way may not be pretty, but it is an expression of intense concentration. It can't be like watching a baseball game. You need to be free of distractions in order to absorb what is happening in the video.

Next, you need to **visualize** yourself skiing like the people in the videos. As discussed on page 26 of this book, you will benefit most if you do these visualizations just after you retire for the evening, and right before you get out of bed in the morning. There is a significant amount of research on this subject that suggests this is the best time to learn from visualization, because you are less frantic and more relaxed. As you lay in bed, picture yourself making a series of turns just like the people in the videos. Stay with this exercise for a few days and it will become easier. You may need to review the videos each day if you are having trouble creating a complete visualization of yourself skiing like an expert. Study where the skiers in the videos place their hands, and what their legs do to create such a consistent rhythm from turn to turn. It should only take a few minutes each day to do this exercise.

Visualizing yourself as a competent skier is the first step to developing the kind of positive self image that leads you to becoming an expert skier. Seeing yourself as a good skier becomes a very important part of the puzzle. Every time you struggle in your skiing, you should return to a memory of your visualization and think about how good it was and how good you looked in your own mind. Then, you simply remind yourself that you do have what it takes to be a good skier. Believing in yourself enables you to view a series of bad turns as merely an event, neither good nor bad. Your current poor skiing is just a passing event, and now you can look forward to better skiing. Relax, and *search out a more moderate run on which to practice.*

No kidding, take a run on an easy slope. Continuing to beat yourself up on a difficult run, when you are frustrated, takes you further in the wrong direction. Compare this with a run on an easy slope that takes the stress away, allows you to relax, and makes it easier to review the fundamentals. I know this whole visualization concept sounds a bit weird and out-of-the-ordinary, but visualization is a good tool and it will improve your skiing. I suggest you at least try it. It takes even less effort than those exercise devices that promise to make you sleek and slim in just a few minutes a week. Believe me, it is truly a low risk, high reward proposition.

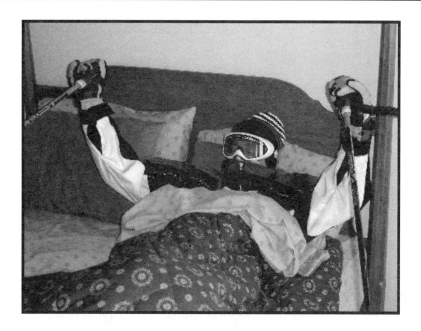

Figure 21.1 *Bed Time Visualization. These mental practice sessions greatly help improve your skiing. The goggles and ski poles aren't really necessary, and be careful not to move your body. This is strictly a mental exercise.*

I do a particular visualization in which I see myself making a series of turns on a groomed run. I see myself making each turn the same, as I imagine myself though each individual turn. It goes like this: I start by standing tall on my skis, driving my ankles forward and slowly increasing the force on my skis until the end of the turn. Then, I stand up tall and start over again. Through the entire visualization I keep my arms in the beach ball position, and I always imagine myself as being very relaxed. You can make it a game by assigning yourself a specific number of turns to make during each visualization session.

You have viewed experts turning correctly, and you have imagined yourself carving great turns. Now it is time to make a **video** of yourself, and play it back in slow motion. As you watch yourself skiing, have a pen and pad handy and makes a few notes about how you see yourself. Note your arm position, how and when you plant your pole, and if you turn the same to each side.

Examples of Written Notes:
1. Arms: held too low, with elbows in close to my side.
2. Pole Plant: occurs late, happening after new turn has started.
3. Turns: good to the left, hesitate to the right.
4. Grip: It appears tight, and I swing my arms to plant my poles.

Written Corrections from Notes:
1. Put arms in beach ball position, with elbows held high.
2. Plant pole at the end of the current turn, to time the new turn.
3. Compare good-side turn to bad side, identify cause and correct. Look for upper body rotation out of the fall line, poor pole plant, dropping one shoulder, etc.
4. Use teacup grip to allow wrist to flick pole. Don't move arm.

Also watch your skis as you descend toward the camera. Are your skis making round turns or do they skid at some point during the turn? After you have studied the video, review the pertinent sections of this book and then practice on the snow by concentrating on correctly applying one body position at a time until it feels natural (Part One of SITS). When each body position no longer feels strange or different, it is then you know you have successfully developed the mind/body engram. It is in your subconscious now and you no longer need to think about it. Practicing the correct body positions makes you a better skier, while practicing the same old, incorrect movements makes you really good at skiing incorrectly. Always remind yourself to stay relaxed, and only practice techniques and body positions on groomed green or blue slopes.

Practicing and learning the correct positions and techniques cleanses your body of bad habits. But, the C in my self-improvement plan stands for **cleansing** the mind of the wrong kind of thinking, and too much thinking about your skiing in general. First, you should learn to think about the right things, and next you should learn not to think: Just do. For example, spending time reminding yourself to relax is a big help, and this is best facilitated by making sure you always use the teacup grip in order to release tension from your upper body. Monitoring your breathing can give you more clues about your current state of mind as you ski. If you are not cycling though a regular and controlled breathing pattern, your skiing will suffer. Be aware of holding your breath or not breathing deeply enough, or not exhaling in and out in a rhythmic cadence. Relax!

It is also helpful not to think negatively about yourself, or to think distracting thoughts. Skiing is expensive, and in and of itself it is a positive experience. Only you can turn it into a frustrating and negative event. I guess the one saving grace (for those of us that have a cocktail or two at the end of skiing) is that by the second drink, the day becomes a great one no matter how we really skied.

We ski best if we are not thinking about how well or how poorly we are doing. If you are absorbed in the moment and not thinking at all, your skiing will look and feel great. I can not tell you how many times I have "come out of the zone" during a great run and started thinking things like, Gee, I am having a great run or, I must look great right now. When I do this I almost always falter and break rhythm, just to see the nice flow I had going fall apart. Your job, as an expert skier, will be to focus on the skiing experience continually unfolding right in front of you, and not to think about anything else.

How and why your mind can have such an influence on your skiing is a vastly complex subject, and we have only scratched the surface in this brief discussion. To get a more complete understanding of how your mind influences your ability to ski, I recommend you pick up a copy of Tim Gallwey and Robert Kreigel's book *Inner Skiing.*

Lastly, get rhythm by following an expert on a groomed run. I suggest you follow someone that is making turns traveling at a moderate speed. Do not try to fall in behind a supercarver traveling at 30 to 50 miles per hour.

Follow at a safe distance, and mimic each turn the accomplished skier makes. This will immediately help you understand the rhythm of the carved turn dance you should be doing, as you ski down the slope.

CHAPTER 22

PROGRESSIVE MUSCLE RELAXATION

It seems like every time someone is trying to show you how to do something new, the most frequent comment you hear is, "Just relax and it will be easy." That is true, but most people are unable to turn relaxation on and off just because someone asks them to do it.

In the world of skiing, relaxation is a very black and white subject. You are either relaxed or you are tense. When skiing, being tense completely disrupts your ability to use the correct techniques to get down the mountain. Tension tightens your muscles, causing you to adapt a static body position. This disables your lower body's capacity to use flexion and extension, and as a result, you are unable to carve turns and control the terrain as you ski.

With a relaxed body and mind, you involuntarily exclude the tension that causes tight muscles. The benefit of being in a relaxed state when skiing is that you feel almost no anxiety and your body is able to move freely from turn to turn, making the necessary up and down movements required for good skiing. Once you learn how your muscles feel when relaxed, it is a matter of practice to bring them into this tension-free state.

Relaxation can be taught through the application of a simple exercise in which you progressively relax all the major muscle groups in your body. This exercise can be done in just a few minutes in almost any place: on the chairlift, in the lodge, or in your kitchen. It is a tool you can quickly grasp and use to reduce your anxiety level when skiing.

However, this relaxation tool is not for everyone. If you have a type of thought disorder that distorts reality, you should avoid relaxation techniques. This would include people with schizophrenia and other forms of psychosis. Generally, relaxation techniques are very safe, but if you feel any discomfort from doing the following exercise you should stop it immediately.

Using a progressive muscle relaxing technique will teach you to achieve deep muscular relaxation through a sequential tensing and releasing of your major muscle groups.

Muscle Relaxation Technique

Sit upright in a stable chair that will not slide along the floor. Make yourself comfortable, and place both feet flat on the floor in front of you. Begin by lifting and straightening your legs in front of you. While holding your legs parallel to the floor, flex your calves and quadriceps as you move your feet toward you. Keep your leg muscles flexed and hold this position for a five count, followed by pointing your feet away from your body. Continue to hold for an additional five count, and then relax. Let you legs go back slowly as you place them in their original position. With your feet resting on the floor, relax all the muscles in your feet, calves, and thighs. Feel the sensation of your legs being completely relaxed. This comfortable sensation comes up from your toes, though your calves, and into your quadriceps. You are feeling very relaxed and calm.

The upper body is next, starting with your arms. From the sitting position, stretch out your arms and make two fists. Make sure your fists are clenched tightly, with pressure on your fingers. Hold the clench for a five count, and relax. Return your arms to their original resting position on your lap and enjoy the feeling of relaxation for 10 or 15 seconds. At this point, return your arms to the stretched position in front of you and tighten up your wrists, lower arms, and upper arms. Hold your arms tight for a five count, while your hands are open. Return your arms to their original position and relax. Once again, spend 10 or 15 seconds enjoying the sensation of being calm and relaxed. Your sense of calm can be further enhanced if you close your eyes during the relaxation segment.

The next step tightens the facial muscles. Start with the forehead by raising the muscles just above the eyes to tighten them. While holding this position, also tighten the muscles around your eyes. Hold for a five count and relax. Pull your eyebrows down, and frown hard for a five count, and then close your eyelids tightly. Feel the tension develop around your eyes and up into your forehead. Relax for 10 to 15 seconds. Next press your tongue against the roof of your mouth and experience the pressure, followed by relaxing your mouth. Purse your lips into an "O", hold for a five count and release. Briefly close your eyes and feel your entire face relaxing.

Moving on to the neck area, press your head as far back as you can without discomfort. Hold for a five count and experience the tension in your neck. From this position gently drop your head forward and slowly roll it to the right, as if looking over your shoulder slightly. Repeat this head movement over your left shoulder. Hold your head in each direction just long enough to feel stress move and then disappear as you continue with each position. Take 10 - 15 seconds to relax, and then bend your head forward until your chin touches or comes close to your chest. Feel the tension in the back of your neck. Hold this position for a five count and relax. Return you head to its normal upright position, lift your shoulders up high (like a shrug) and hold for a five count. Relax the shoulders, and feel your throat, neck and shoulders become very relaxed.

To finish, return to your relaxed sitting position, with your arms resting in your lap. Begin to breathe in through your nose, slowly, and deeply. Hold your breath for just a second or two while flexing your stomach and chest muscles. Release the air slowly through pursed lips, as you let go of all your anxiety and your tension. Do only two to three repetitions of this breathing exercise, being careful not to hyperventilate.

To complete the exercise, do a quick scan of your body. Do you feel any tension? Let it flow out of you, and continue to relax. You are ready to ski. Stop at the top of your chosen run, feel the relaxation throughout your body, and ease into the first turn with confidence.

Do not do this exercise while riding the chairlift unless it has a safety bar and foot rest you can lower into position. It is not imperative you do this exercise right before you ski. I found it to be very helpful if I did it the night before, and/or in the morning before leaving for the ski hill. This progressive relaxation technique worked quite well for me if I stopped before each run and reviewed the feeling of relaxation I experienced during the exercise earlier in the day.

For years, I used this technique to get rid of the pre-competition butterflies, and it successfully got my feet back on the ground so I could actually feel them in the starting gate. Below I have reiterated the sequence of this progressive exercise as a numerical list. This should make it easier to follow.

PROGRESSIVE MUSCLE RELAXATION EXERCISE

1. **Begin by sitting in a stable unpadded chair.**

2. **Stretch legs out in front of you, with arms in lap.**
    a. Flex calf and quad muscles, and hold.
    b. Move feet and toes toward your head. Hold for 5 seconds.
    c. Point feet away. Hold additional 5 seconds.
    d. Relax, and slowly put feet back on floor.
    e. Continue to relax all leg muscles.
    f. Feel the sensation of relaxation flow up from the toes.

3. **Stretch out your arms and make fists with each hand.**
   a. Clench tightly, hold for 5 seconds.
   b. Return arms to lap and relax for 10 -15 seconds.
   c. Stretch arms out in front of you.
   d. With hands open, flex wrists, lower arms, and upper arms
   e. Hold arms tight for 5 seconds.
   f. Return arms to lap and relax for 10 -15 seconds.

4. **Tighten facial muscles, starting with forehead.**
   a. Raise eyebrows to flex forehead muscles, and hold.
   b. Close eyelids hard, hold for 5 seconds.
   d. Relax eyebrows and open eyes. Relax for 10 -15 seconds.
   e. Press tongue against roof of mouth.
   f. Hold for 5 seconds, and then relax.
   g. Purse lips into "O", hold for 5 seconds, and relax.
   h. Briefly close eyes and feel entire face relaxing.

5. **Press your head back to tighten neck and shoulder muscles.**
   a. Gently, hold head back 5 seconds. Feel tension in neck.
   b. Drop head forward and roll to right looking over shoulder.
   c. Hold this position a few seconds, feel tension and release.
   d. Repeat to the left. Hold to feel tension and release.
   e. Relax for 10 -15 seconds.
   f. Bend head forward; try to rest the chin on chest.
   g. Feel the tension in the back of the neck.
   h. Hold this position for 5 seconds, and then relax.
   i Return head to upright position, lift shoulders up high.
   j. Hold for 5 seconds.
   k. Relax the shoulders and feel your throat, neck, and shoulders
   become very relaxed.

6. **Finish with a breathing exercise.**
   a. Breath in through your nose, slowly, and deeply.
   b. Do not exhale, instead hold breath for 1- 2 seconds.
   c. While holding breath, flex stomach and chest muscles.
   d. Now, release air slowly through pursed lips.
   e. Feel anxiety and tension leave through lips.
   f. Repeat only two or three times, don't hyperventilate.

7. Mentally scan body for tension.
      a. Do you feel any tension?
      b. Let it flow out of you, and continue to relax.

We suggest you practice this progressive exercise with a goal of committing it to memory. Once you know it, you can quickly move through the exercise. Doing the exercise without hesitation between muscle groups increases the benefit. When it becomes second nature to move through the entire relaxation technique you will be able to purge more and more tension from your body.

Relaxation techniques slow down the body and quiet the mind, which helps promote long-term health. These exercises increase body awareness and focus your attention away from stress. If you would like to know more about relaxation techniques you can search the internet under the following headings: Autogenic Training, Progressive Muscle Relaxation, and Meditation.

You Are Only as Good as the Weakest Link

CHAPTER 23

CORRECT ALIGNMENT IS FIRST

Most of my ski career I have recommended custom foot beds to all my friends. Footbeds are the first step in making sure your body is aligned above your skis, establishing a balanced stance.

Customer Foot Beds

To develop the correct stance on your skis, start with custom footbeds. This begins the process of building a perfect skier and equipment interface. The goal is to stand in perfect balance over your skis and be able to efficiently and quickly edge your skis, shift your weight, and move from turn to turn with a minimum of effort.

This requires that your feet, ankles, lower legs, knees, and hips are stacked on top of your skis in such a way that your ski runs flat on the snow until you move to engage the edge. If you are misaligned, you will always be riding skis that are on edge to some degree. And, guess what? Shape skis really exaggerate this problem due to their propensity to easily tip on edge. If you seem to be on edge all the time, and you are knock-kneed or bowlegged, this is a sure sign you should seek out an alignment assessment from a professional. The place to start looking for a professional boot-fitter is at your local specialty ski shop.

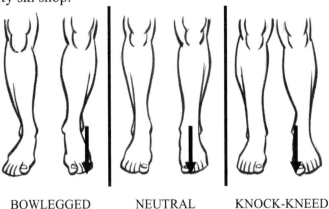

BOWLEGGED   NEUTRAL   KNOCK-KNEED

Figure 23.1 *Left to Right: Bowlegged, Neutral, and Knock-kneed. The arrows indicate where the foot puts pressure on the ski. Only in the neutral position will the ski run flat when not being edged.*

The essential components of a good alignment are custom foot-beds, an upper cuff adjustment, and fore-aft balancing. It all starts with your feet and ankles. Your first step is to get a custom foot-bed that places you foot in its natural position. Footbeds that are formed using a semi or non-weight-bearing process do this best in my opinion. Although, the best boot fitters can probably make a weight-bearing process work well for you.

Before you have your footbeds made, take time to talk to the technician, and communicate any past problems you have had with foot pain, abnormal wear patterns on your shoes, or personal alignment issues.

Upper Cuff Adjustment

Once your foot-bed is completed, it is time to get an upper cuff adjustment for your ski boots. This adjustment correctly positions your leg in the boot cuffs. Remove your boot liners and step into your shells to begin the assessment. Typically, your legs are positioned in your upper boot cuffs directly in the center, slanted to the left, or slanted to the right. If you are not positioned in the center of your cuffs, you need a lateral upper-cuff adjustment. This will position your legs so they do not press against either side of your cuffs. With your lower legs centered, it will not pressure your ski edges inadvertently. You can align your boot cuffs at home, but until you completely understand how to do it, we suggest you allow your local ski shop or boot-fitter to do it for you. If you purchased your boots from them, they will probably do it at no charge.

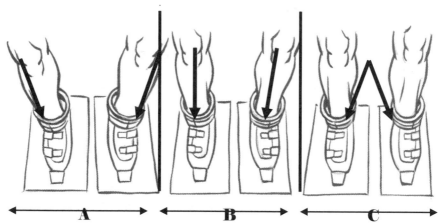

Figure 23.2 *Proper Leg and Upper Cuff Alignment:* *From left to right, legs are pressing against the outside of the cuff (A), legs are centered in the cuff (B is correct), and legs are pressing against the inside of the cuff (C). To be able to edge the skis quickly and precisely the legs must be centered in the upper boot cuff.*

A custom foot-bed and an upper cuff alignment should be enough to get you into a balanced stance over your skis. Now, when riding a flat ski it should be without any compensating movement from you. Best of all, when you do edge your ski, it will happen more quickly and precisely than before your custom boot fitting. If however; you still seem to struggle, you may need further alignment. This involves using some type of plumb bob device to verify you are aligned, and may also involve re-adjusting your upper cuffs a bit. See your boot fitting professional for details.

There are other factors that may inhibit you from achieving proper alignment. One side of your lower body may be different from the other, or you may have one leg that is shorter. Correcting these situations usually requires a trained professional, such as a orthopedic specialist or podiatrist.

As you journey down the alignment path, you can check your progress by doing a simple on-snow drill. We recommend that you do this drill before you make any changes in your alignment, and then repeat the drill after each major change. This will give you feedback on which changes helped the most, and also if you need to continue to making changes.

We refer to this drill as the One-Legged Flamingo Drill. It will help you evaluate your current ability to balance yourself on skis, and determine if you may have an alignment problem.

ONE-LEGGED FLAMINGO DRILL ON SNOW

1. Pick a very flat, smooth beginner run.
2. Point your skis straight down the hill, and let them run slowly.
3. Now do like the Flamingo, pick up one leg (ski) and try to ride the other ski straight down this gentle slope without moving your upper body.
5. If you are tipsy, just spread your wings for balance, or in this case, your arms.
6. If you are correctly aligned you will track straight without your skis edging.
7. If you have to constantly reposition your arms and body to keep the ski going straight, then – Houston, we have a problem!
8. Ok, remember what happened on the first foot and try it on the other foot.
9. If you had difficulty maintaining your balance on either foot, you are mostly likely a candidate for a custom boot alignment.

**Your local ski specialty shop can help you
get your boots and/or body aligned.**

Even if you don't think you need a custom boot alignment, we strongly recommend you explore the idea. There won't be a cost to have an exploratory conversation with a professional boot-fitter. If an alignment makes you a better skier, you will get your investment back many times over. We are betting you save a lot of money from not buying equipment that you hoped would make you a better skier. As long as your current equipment is in good working order, and of the modern variety, you will not be thinking about new purchases. You will just be enjoying skiing. You will be pleasantly surprised how well your current equipment works if your body is properly aligned.

Fore-Aft Alignment

Another element of alignment that affects your skiing is your fore-aft stance. When you are correctly positioned fore and aft, you should stand tall on your skis with no real effort. You should be gently supported by your boot tongues and able to relax in this position. If you do not have your weight riding slightly against your boot tongue, you will constantly struggle to be perfectly positioned as you ski over subtle variations in the terrain. When positioned correctly, the angle of your lower leg should match the angle of your lower back as you ski down the hill. This is illustrated by the skier on the right in Figure 5.1, page 31.

Part of what creates a proper fore-aft stance is the ramp angle of your ski boots. If a boot has no ramp built into it, then your heel and the ball of your foot are on the same horizontal plane, or level to each other. But if your boots have ramp angle built into them (and most do) your heel rests higher than the ball of your foot. Your bindings also have ramp angle or lack of it, built into them. Together they can make up various combinations of a total ramp angle. It is your job to get the right combination for you. To get this right remember that when you are standing tall in your boots and bindings, several things need to happen: your lower legs are resting comfortably against the front of your boots, you can stand tall without effort, your legs are relaxed, and the angle of your lower leg matches the angle of your lower back when you stand on your skis. If you are too far forward when standing in your boots it will be necessary for you to expend effort to hold the position, and you won't be able to completely relax.

Inspect your bindings and your boots for ramp angle to decide what combination works for you. One thing to consider when accessing your ramp angle needs is how you stand naturally. To do this, stand barefooted on a wood or tiled floor. Look straight ahead and stand naturally, while feeling how your weight is distributed on your feet. Is it divided equally between the balls of your feet and your heels? Or do you stand with more weight on your heels, like I do? Or, maybe you have more weight on the balls of your feet. Knowing how your weight is distributed will help you decide on a ramp angle. If you naturally stand with the weight on your heels, you will need more ramp angle in your boots to account for this, or your weight may shift onto the back of your skis more than you wish.

Better ski shops have the means to assess your fore-aft needs, and the ones that know their business will put you though a litany of tests and questions in order to help you. They will use tools like a balance board, calipers, shims, and heel lifts, just to mention a few. Be aware that some boots have more ramp than others, and some bindings have more ramp than others. Specialist in the ski industry can help you get it right.

CHAPTER 24

BOOTS, SKIS, AND BINDINGS

An audiophile once told me that a music system is only as good as its weakest link. He said that if you buy an inexpensive amplifier, and combine it with the most expensive speakers; they will only produce an inexpensive sound.

We believe this to be true in both music and skiing. You will only ski as well as your weakest link. If you buy powder skis and racing boots, in most cases you will never be much more than a mediocre powder skier and a very bad racer.

Be careful! Spend time, and do your homework before you decide to buy. Making a list of your intended uses for the equipment always helps. But, to get this right requires honesty and future vision on your part. Decide what types of snow and terrain you want to ski most of the time, and purchase accordingly. You can also throw awareness into the mix. You need to be aware of what each different boot or ski is designed to do. This is tricky territory because a sales person in the local store may not be knowledgeable enough to give you good information.

Industry magazines, such as *Ski*, *Skiing*, and *Powder* are great reference guides to help you decide on gear choices. If you read the mountains of data they present to you very carefully, you will know what the intended use is for a particular piece of equipment. Combine this with relentless interrogation of friends, family, and experts; and you should be ready to make some meaningful choices.

Let me give you an idea of my thought process on this subject. I like to ski everywhere on the mountain, and in all snow conditions. So, for me a good ski choice is the all-mountain expert ski. I use a ski technique that requires a lot of flexing at the ankle, and I ski best in boots that have a relative soft forward flex. Yet, I like an instant transfer of power from my boot to my ski edge; requiring I have a boot that is very stiff laterally. Oh, I also most forgot to tell you I also have a thin flat foot. Because of this, I like a very low volume boot that will be easier to custom fit to my low volume foot. If you buy a boot that is too big for your foot you can stuff a lot of padding in it to take up the extra space, but this just creates other problems. Get a boot that has been designed with your foot shape in mind.

I have many friends that ski on an all mountain ski and a soft flexing boot, yet they seem to be able to perform like an expert everywhere. If your technique is good, an all mountain ski will allow you to ski fast on the groomers. Then you can use the same ski to jump into the moguls or powder. But, it doesn't work very well to take a racing or carving ski off the groomed runs. These skis are not intended to ski powder, moguls, or trees.

To confuse matters even more, ski manufacturers have responded to the market by coming out with numerous sub-categories of ski models in recent years. All these new market segments are too many and too varied to talk about here. But, we thought it might be fun just to see the list we compiled from various magazines here and abroad.

1) **Freeride XL**
2) **Freeride XXL**
3) **Women-specific**
4) **All-Mountain Expert: Freeride**
5) **All-Mountain Expert: Speed**
6) **One-Ski Quiver Expert**
7) **Big Mountain Freestyle**
8) **Backcountry Freestyle**
9) **Big Mountain Freeride**
10) **All Mountain Cruiser**
11) **Aspiring Expert**
12) **Frontside**
13) **Race**
14) **Carving**
15) **Powder**
16) **Deep Powder**
17) **Powder: Reverse sidecut, Reverse Camber**
18) **Pipe and Park**
19) **Off-Piste**
20) **Big Mountain Pro/Custom**

If any list ever epitomized good news, bad news, this is it! Obviously, the bad news is there are way too many choices. The good news is there are a lot of great choices. In recent years, ski manufacturers have moved outside the proverbial "nine dots" and have designed many fabulous skis, giving you numerous choices from within one category, and some will work well for you.

Handling this "choice" situation requires some thought and planning on your part if you want to pick the ski that best suits your skiing desires. If you are going to take advantage of demo days at your local area, you will want to make it well worth your time. To do that, you must have some idea of what feedback you are looking for from a ski. For example, if it is an All-Mountain variety, you should chart a course through the crud, moguls, and hard snow, at the very least. Be sure to take every demo ski through the same terrain. It's best to be systematic in your approach to testing new skis. One caveat: You may not want to make a buying decision based on one day's test. I have done it, and I can summarize the experience by saying I wish I had that $750.00 back. I tried two different skis on the same day in identical conditions. The problem with this scenario was that the snow condition I most often skied was missing that day. As luck would have it, the ski I chose was not great for my favorite type of white stuff. Now, I always try to test a ski for **my** intended purpose before I buy it. Duh!

Generally speaking, there are few things to consider when buying skis. First, when a ski is very wide at the waist it takes longer to get the ski on edge. Therefore, skis that are wide at the tip, tail, and waist made longer radius turns. Another way to put it is to say these skis turn slower than skis with narrower waists. If you don't like fast turning squirrelly skis you should avoid narrow-waisted skis. Other skis do everything with quiet aplomb, yet they never give you back that high energy feedback you may lust for when the ripping gets good. For me, I prefer a ski that is quick, agile, and full of energy. On the other hand, I love to ski powder as much as I love to cruise the groomers. To find a ski that does everything well, I usually end up with an all mountain style ski sporting a narrower waist than others in the category.

If you look at modern skis, most of the time you will see a number representing the width of the tip, tail, and waist stamped on it, accompanied by a number that represents the sidecut radius. These numbers most often appear on the top side of the back of the ski or on the side of the ski. For example, we ski on all-mountain expert skis that have numbers in the area of 116 (tip), 78 (waist), and 105 (tail). These numbers represent the width at each of these three points on the ski, and are expressed in millimeters. Interestingly, we ski on boards with sidecut radii from 16m to 30m, however the entire range for all skis is approximately 13m (Carving Skis) through 34m (Big Mountain Pro/Custom). The sidecut radius is expressed in meters (m), and *the smaller this number the tighter the ski will turn.*

When thinking of purchasing skis, it is also important to remember choosing a width can be a geographic decision. In the Western United States, a skier can spend most of the season on a mid-fat ski. But go east, and you will only see skis this wide on a powder day. I guess the moral of that statement is; don't buy your skis for conditions typical in the East, and then ski on them in the West. Surprisingly, that was a dilemma for traveling skiers at one time when rental shops carried lower quality skis and boots. Now, however, rental shops carry high quality ski equipment. This eliminates the need to travel with your own skis, and it provides a great opportunity to try new boards.

To help you make a more educated choice, we have laid out a compatibility chart as a general guide line to help make your gear decisions.

Type of Ski	Intended Use	Compatible Boot
One-Ski Quiver Expert	Ski everywhere, best choice if you only get one pair.	High Performance, not Ultra High Performance. Many experts get away with skiing a "performance" boot. (less money, more comfort)
All Mountain Expert	The name says it all. Intended to go almost anywhere. First love is soft snow. Exception; very hard snow.	Soft forward flex, stiff laterally, comfortable.
Big Mountain	For descending (you guessed it) big mtns. Straight down big scary lines.	Race cuff support, with comfort fit for slogging to the top of walk-up summits
Powder Specific	Powder and almost nothing else.	All mtn boots or one step down. Soft forward flex is essential for powder skiing.
Racing	Race Course, high speed on hard snow	Race boot.
Carving	Firm, or hard, or very hard snow.	Race boot

If you look at Figure 24.1 on page 191 you can see there is a substantial difference in the widths of these skis. The big mountain model is very wide, but also differs in side cut from the others. You will notice it has a very shallow sidecut when compared to the carving ski profile. To better understand the differences in the shapes of skis, you can think of sidecut as the hourglass profile that the skis present when you look straight at them. The four ski shapes depicted in Figure 24.1 have very different functions as indicated in the above chart under "intended uses."

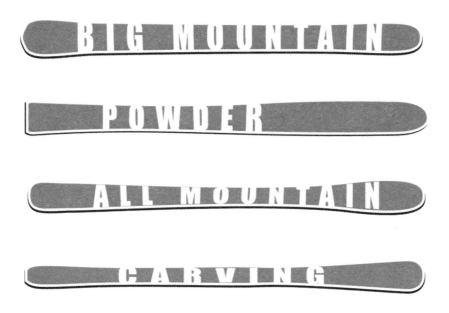

Figure 24.1 Ski Shapes: *The Big Mountain Ski is the widest, allowing it to stay on top of the snow when descending big open slopes. The Powder Ski is also a wide ski to provide floatation, but sinks more than the Big Mountain Ski. The All Mountain Ski has more side cut to work in a wider range of conditions. Carving Skis have the most sidecut, enabling them to make quick, short turns on firm snow.*

IN OUR OPINION

In our opinion there are some general assumptions you can make about ski gear. Our opinions have been formed from years of experience in many areas of the ski industry. These opinions were developed in direct correlation to the equipment we use to ski in all conditions, on a variety of terrain.

1) Always try before you buy. This should be the unbreakable rule.

2) You must flex your ankle to ski correctly. Buy a boot that has a softer forward flex.

3) Shorter skis work better. (This is true to a point.)

4) Function before fashion. We are color un-coordinated. To us, it makes more sense to buy equipment that works, rather than equipment that coordinates well with our clothing, boots, or whatever.

5) Goggles rule, and sun glasses are a deck tool. The glasses look good at lunch, but goggles make life easier on the slope (and safer).

6) If you are on a budget, it's ok to buy last year's gear. After all, it is better than all the ski equipment ever made except for this year's gear.

7) Technical Wear: Is there any other kind of ski clothing?

8) Layering your clothing; very smart! Polypro T-shirt, Polypro T-neck, Optional vest (when it's really cold), Shell Jacket, Shell Pants. Heavier layering is advisable if you don't ski hard and long.

9) When you wear a helmet, you can put your goggles up and they won't fog. When you're wearing a hat, don't put your goggles up on your head – they will fog every time.

10) Helmets are warmer and cooler. (They have vents you can open and close.) We always wear them, mainly to avoid the dreaded goggle gap.

There are many great equipment choices on the market today, and all you need to do is match your real needs with the right equipment.

A Word about Bindings

Fat skis are getting really fat! In fact, it is a phenomenon occurring for all types of skis, and this has happened fast causing binding manufacturers to play catch-up. Bindings once lacked both width and rigidity, but that is no longer the case. The bindings out this year have the right stuff. The fact is, bindings have been really good for some time now, and the newer models are even better. Enough said.

Chapter 25

POLES, HELMETS, GLOVES, GOGGLES

Helmets, gloves, and goggles are important ancillaries to the equipment chain, but none are as important as poles. Poles are one of the three primary tools in skiing, along with your boots and skis. It is important for you to get the right length and shape, combined with the correct grip. These three components must also be built into a pole that has a light swing weight. All together they make up a pole that will improve your skiing.

During our discussion of pole length in Part Two, on page 49 and 50, we did not talk about pole styles. Style is important, and we don't go anywhere without stylish ski poles that help us survive long, hard days. When you are skiing 25,000 vertical feet through big, steep bumps in just four hours; you will begin to appreciate your poles if they are light and swing back and forth easily.

Poles Matter:

In my humble opinion, the right pole for everyone *is an expensive one*. Sorry, but if you don't skimp here you will thank me later. There are three things you should look for in a high quality ski pole. First, make sure it has an offset grip. To determine if offset is present in the grip, hold the pole by the shaft so the grip is just above eye level. Look to see if the grip is mounted straight onto the shaft or if it resides at a slight angle to the shaft. If it is an offset grip you will not be able to draw an imaginary straight line up the shaft through the center of the grip. An offset grip is titled forward on the shaft (fig. 25.1 on page 194), and this enables you to make quicker pole plants.

Your next task is to look for a grip that is arched on the back or palm side of the grip (fig. 25.1). This arch makes it easier for you to flick the pole back and forth using a teacup grip (remember, the little finger and ring finger are not holding on). Choosing a pole made of a metal matrix or carbon material is best.

Finally, you want to consider swing weight. This is an interesting subject, as it is a bit more complicated than just choosing the lightest pole in the place. Swing weight is determined by the grip and the weight distribution over the length of the pole. Poles that are designed with a grip that offsets your hand from the shaft, and are lighter at the top and heavier at the bottom, will exhibit a light swing weight. Flicking these poles out and back, as in a pole plant, feels effortless compared to an inexpensive pole (think low end or rental). Even though the pole shaft and basket are heavier than the top of the pole and grip, it still whips out from your hand with ease due to the pendulum effect. Remember, this style of ski pole will quicken your plant. It also takes less effort, and this is critical when you are trying to hold your hands out in front of your body for hours.

A pole with a light swing weight speeds up everything you do when skiing. Obviously, it makes your pole plants quicker, but it also helps you turn faster (as in more times per minute), and you can ski faster longer because it takes less energy output to manage than a heavier pole. Who would have thought it? Next time you are in a ski shop swing all their poles, and you will notice a difference. The one that feels the lightest will be the most expensive.

Figure 25.1 *This Pole has a Side-Arched, Offset Grip that Facilitates Flicking it Out in Front of You. It also encourages the teacup grip. Due to the grip shape, it is difficult to grab with all four fingers and your thumb. High quality poles will have small baskets and a very light swing weight.*

194

Helmets

Let's see: They come with ventilation systems, removable liners, and built-in headphones. What is there not to like? Some are Bluetooth functional, with separate in-put devices for your avalanche beacon, and many weigh less than 10 ounces nicely equipped.

Want to put your goggles up and soak in more sunshine on the lift? No problem; helmets don't let any heat escape from your head in the area where your goggles will be resting. Then, there is the creme de la creme; a helmet that sucks fog up into it and out the back via a rotating wheel regulator. Most helmets have adjustable vents that can be manipulated with your gloves on. Hats and helmets both smash your hair, but only the latter offers protection.

Gloves

On powder days we wish everyone wore those cheap gloves, causing them to go in the lodge more often. Gloves should fit snugly, but not tight. Adjustments need to be easily made with your gloves on. It should have a closure mechanism at the cuff that can be manipulated without taking your other glove off. If you have habitually cold hands, you can find gloves with small pockets for concealing heat packets. When faced with a lot of options, we choose simplicity, and never buy gloves touted as being able to do it all. Last but not least, you will want to buy a glove that accomplishes the correct interface with your ski jacket. The question is; should the cuff go inside your jacket or over the outside? What did your mother always do when she put your mittens on? Do the opposite (on everything else mother's know best).

Goggles

Let's face it, sun glasses may look cooler, but when you ski fast, or in powder or trees, their lack of protection becomes an issue. Goggles, on the other hand, offer protection from the elements and clear vision in the toughest of conditions. Today's goggles take it a step further; offering funky styles, the latest fashion colors, and most are compatible with helmets.

When purchasing your goggles, take your lid with you to ensure compatibility. Some goggles and helmets cannot be worn together. The other important consideration when purchasing goggles is to choose a frame size that fits your face. With the goggles on your face, you should not be able to see light leaking in around the edges, and the nose recess must fit snugly against the contours of your nose. *Goggles with spherically shaped lenses will give you a higher quality of vision and more peripheral vision.*

Finally, goggles always enhance your vision the most when the lens is matched to the light conditions of the day. When the light is flat, you will see the definition in the snow more clearly with a yellow lens. Darker lens are nice for sunny days, and mirrored coatings help keep glare out. Try to purchase goggles that come with more than one lens or you may want to buy two pairs; one with a light lens and one with a dark lens.

To look your best in goggles never allow a gap to develop between your hat, or helmet, and the top of your goggle. The worst scenario is when you have some frozen or wet hair sticking out of the gap! (Not pretty.)

CHAPTER 26

THE FIVE MINUTE SKI TUNE

To start this section I am providing you with a laundry list of turning problems; some of which we all experience from time to time. These problems are typically caused by an array of skier issues ranging from a technical flaw to being a misaligned skier, with a plethora of other causes in between. Yet, everything on this list can also be caused by a single problem: ***POORLY TUNED SKIS.***

1) **Difficulty in starting turns.**
2) **Catching edges frequently.**
3) **Skis skid and wander instead of running straight.**
4) **Skis won't hold an edge on ice.**
5) **Difficulty holding a consistent arc through the turn.**
6) **Skis are slow, and seem to stick to the snow.**
7) **Yours friends leave you behind on cat tracks.**

Informal surveys conducted at major U.S. ski resorts suggest that at any given time, nearly 70% of the skiers have poorly tuned skis. I am guessing that explains why so many skiers are controlled by the terrain they are skiing over, instead of the other way around. But, why not keep your skis tuned?

Some skiers actually avoid tuning their skis because they think it will make them go too fast. Another group of non-tuners think it isn't necessary because the skis are new, or were tuned in the last three or four months. Isn't tuning your skis once a year enough? No, it is a nightly ritual for expert skiers, and it only takes five minutes.

If you tune your skis each time before you ski, *you will always ski better.* Tuning your skis this frequently sounds like it can be time consuming and expensive, but that is not the case. If the area where you ski is having a decent snow year, you probably only need to take your skis to the shop a few times each year. For the rest of the season, you can tune your skis at home in a few minutes, and they will stay in top-notch shape. However, this is dependent on two variables. First, you need to tune your bases correctly to avoid ending up with a ski that is even worse than before you started. Second, you should make a conscious effort to avoid rocks when skiing.

Making sure you start with skis that are perfectly tuned is essential, and is precisely why you should take them to a ski or tuning shop for the initial base and edge setup. While at the shop, take time to have a pre-tune conversation with the person that will be working on your skis. The shop technician will begin by checking the flatness of your ski base. If the base is convex or concave, the technician will machine grind your skis flat (only a flat ski turns easily and correctly). Then, through a cooperative effort, the two of you need to decide about tip and tail dulling, edge bevel, base structure, and the type of wax. There may also be talk of preparing your skis specifically for today's snow conditions. Let's take each of these discussion points and explore them one at a time.

For the general skiing public, dulling of the tips and tails is a thing of the past, as dulling died when shape skis arrived. Shape skis only need to be detuned in the rarest of situations now, unless you want to dull the first few inches of the tips and tails for safety reasons. This may save you from a facial or other laceration if you windmill down the slopes with your skis flying around you.

The only other time detuning will be required is if you have the old style skis. For these, dull the tips and tails back only to the start of the ski's running surface when pressed flat. To determine this, simply put the ski on a hard, level counter top or floor and press it flat and hold it there. Note where the edges near the tip and tail no longer touch the surface under the ski base, and have your skis dulled from that point out to the end of the tip and the tail.

Next, you want to decide on an edge bevel appropriate for you. This will include deciding on a base edge bevel and a side edge bevel. This is where honesty is the best policy. Confess to the ski technician your true ability as a skier, and they will set up your edge bevels accordingly. A base edge bevel typically ranges from 2-degrees down to .5-degrees for expert skiers. If you are an intermediate skier you will want to choose a base bevel around 1-degree, but not less.

With that decided, it is time to make a decision about the side edge bevel. This is an easy choice, as for almost all recreational skiers a 1-degree side bevel will work just fine. Hard core racers, traveling at high speeds on icy courses, can require as much as a 3-degree side bevel. Don't even think about it. After you have agreed on some bevel numbers write them down and tuck them safely away. Many shops will place a small sticker on your skis with your bevel numbers written on it.

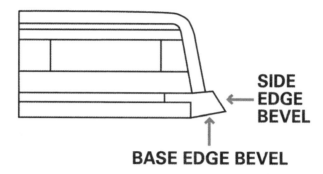

SIDE ← EDGE BEVEL

BASE EDGE BEVEL

Figure 26.1 *Cut Away View of Ski: showing base-edge bevel and side-edge bevel.*

Structuring your skis involves using a stone grinder that puts a pattern on the base. It can be thought of as a very shallow design that is cut or scraped into the base of your ski. You must tip the base toward the light just to see the faint pattern imposed on the ski. A design that is tight with few spaces between the ridges works best in dry snow, while a wider spaced pattern will work nicely in wet snow. Generally speaking, structuring a ski's base enables it to channel water crystals to the sides and tail of the ski, resulting in a much faster ski. Structured bases also are more resistant to small impacts without scratching, and it prepares the ski to more readily accept wax.

As a final step in the tuning process, many shops apply a universal wax by quickly passing the base of your ski through a hot-wax machine. It is debatable as to whether or not this type of application actually bonds the wax to your base. More likely, in most cases it just sticks on top of your bases and wears off during the day, and most certainly it will be gone in several days. Actually, this does not matter in my way of thinking. I have a more esoteric viewpoint of the whole waxing game. A good wax job matters most at the beginning of your ski day. Here's why; if your skis are waxed they initiate into the turn more easily, glide down the cat tracks faster, and allow you to generally feel freer on your skis because less friction exists between your skis and the snow. Your skis just feel lighter when properly waxed. This gives a great start to your ski day. Who cares if the wax wears off half way through the day? My rhythm has been established early, as I started the day feeling light on my skis and melted snow with some "smokin" turns. The key is to make sure your skis are ready to go every morning you ski. The edges may only need a touch up, and smearing any amount of wax on your skis is better than nothing. Now imagine there was a method to tune your skis that actually gave you a great result and prepped your skis for the day in just five to ten minutes. You're in luck, for just such a tune exists, and it will help your skiing immensely if you are not tuning regularly. This is a tune you can do at home on a regular basis, and it will help your shop tune last a long time.

Five Minute Tune (It's more like a touch-up.)

This is really only a touch-up you will be doing to your ski bases, and it requires very few special tools. You will need a bar of universal wax, a few stout rubber bands, a file, and a cork. You can get all your tuning supplies at a ski or tune shop. In addition, it is helpful to have a ski vise, but not necessary. Without the vise you will need to be creative and devise a way to secure your ski so you can work on it without injuring yourself. I have successfully touched up my skis in many hotel rooms without a vise, and without damage to the room or myself. Not everyone has been as careful as I have, and today many hotels do not allow skis in the room. But, we are now seeing the development of tuning rooms in the common areas of lodging establishments. I always ask about this when I make a reservation. Touching up your skis at home or away is easy. The following six steps tell you how to do the five minute touch up on your ski bases, and doing it will make your skiing more enjoyable instantly.

1) Clean any dirt, tree pitch, grease or other debris off the bases of your skis.

2) Secure your ski brakes in the up position with your stout rubber bands. Use one band per brake by capturing one brake arm and then stretching the band over your ski top and around the other brake arm. This will keep the brakes clear of your edges so you can work on them.

3) *Lightly* run a file along the side edge and this will remove any burrs. Try to hold the file at the same angle as the edge bevel. Remember to do this in only one direction, just cleaning off any burrs you may have pick up while skiing. You are not trying to reset your edge bevel; you are trying to preserve it. Be gentle.

4) Next, take your block of universal wax and rub it up and down your ski until you can see a haze of wax coating the entire ski

base. Put on just enough to create a haze, and do not allow any depth of wax to build up on the ski base.

5) With cork in hand, initially rub the wax into the base with swirl motions. The wax should form small circle shapes the entire length of the ski. Do these circular rubbing motions tip to tail twice, exerting a fair amount of force on the cork. BE CAREFUL – If your hand slips you can receive a nasty cut from your ski edge.

6) To complete the tune-up rub the wax into the base using only a back and forth motion, so that the wax takes on a linear pattern running the length of the ski.

TIP: Your skis should be stored at room temperature overnight to ensure the bases are warm before you hand wax your skis

Professional Tuners may question the validity of this touch-up, but I can tell you from personal experience that it works. A nightly touch up always allows me to start the morning feeling light on my skis, and with a good glide. If you want to improve on the five minute tune, you can keep a variety of waxes on hand and pick the wax best suited to the day's snow temperature.

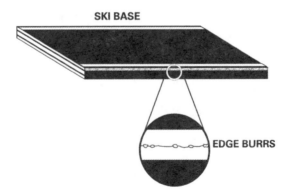

Figure 26.2 *Ski Base with Edge Burrs:* *The circular detail shows a ski edge with burrs. The side and base edge of a ski should always meet in a clean and sharp continuous line, running the length of the ski. A properly sharpened edge feels perfectly smooth to the touch. Check for burrs by running a finger along the edge for the entire length of the ski. Ski edges can be very sharp: be careful not to cut through the skin.*

Ten Minute Tune

This is more than a touch-up; it is more like a quick-tune or a mini-tune. Try to quick-tune your skis every 5 – 7 times you ski, and on the other days you can fill in with the five minute touch up. You will use the same tools from the five minute tune, with the addition of a side edge beveler, a gummi stone, and a medium grit diamond stone. If you purchase a file guide instead of a beveler be sure to get the one that duplicates the side edge bevel you received when the professionals tuned your skis. Remember, you wrote it down and hid it.

Start by repeating steps one and two of the five minute tune and then move on to side-edge beveling. This is best done in a ski vise, and it is really nice to have one that holds your ski on edge, as well as with the base facing up. Another nice addition to your tuning tool kit is a planer that will take away any excess plastic on the ski sidewall that might be getting in your way as you file your side edge. The step by step outline of the ten minute tune is as follows:

1) Place your skis in a vise and secure your brakes in the up position. Clean the dirt and debris off your bases.

2) Take out your handy side edge beveler and place a file in it. Be sure to purchase your file from a ski tool supplier, or at a ski shop. The hardware store variety is too soft. Position your ski upright on its edge in the vise. This provides the best access to your side edges when filing them. Only touch up your side edges, and always leave the base edge beveling to the professionals.

3) As you work on your side edges, bring the beveler toward you in short pulls. To do this keep your arms extended in front of you and back up as you work down the length of the ski. It doesn't matter which way you work down the ski, but don't go both directions when filing. Pick either tip to tail, or tail to tip and stick with it. Don't over file your edges. It helps to color the edge using a black marker before you begin, and quit filing after the black is no longer visible. Note that files only cut in one direction.

4) For this step you will use your diamond stone. Wet the stone with water and place it in your file guide. Run it gently along

the side edge to remove any roughness left by the file. A diamond stone is none directional so you can run it back and forth along the edge. Polishing off your edges will only take a few passes.

5) Finish your edge preparation by gently running your gummi stone along the edge one time to remove any small burrs.

6) Wax your skis following steps four through six in the five minute touch-up.

Don't hesitate to search out more information on ski tuning. At the master level, ski tuning is a precise and complex undertaking. It involves a multi-step process designed to make skis carve more precisely, and go as fast as possible. If you are interested in learning this process check with a specialty tune shop and they will give you information on how to start becoming an expert tuner yourself.

To start this process, you will want to add one tool to your kit immediately. Purchase a true bar to determine if your ski bases are flat. When a true bar is laid across the ski base, no light can be seen between the base and the bar if your ski is flat. To get an accurate assessment, hold the ski on your shoulder, base up, with the tail pointing toward a light source. If you see light seeping between the bar and the base, you have a concave or railed ski. If you see light above the edges, but no light in the middle area of the base, you have a convex ski.

Either base condition causes your skis to turn poorly. When you skis are concave you will be catching edges, and the ski will be more difficult to turn quickly (too much edge contact with the snow). It will also resist directional changes. A convex base makes your skis swim about, and it is difficult to hold the ski on edge through a carved turn (not enough edge contact with the snow). Checking the flatness of your base occasionally will help you avoid either situation. If you keep your skis in good shape, but discover you have concave or convex base, it is an easy fix. Your local shop can grind them flat for a reasonable fee, which can include sharpening your edges and a wax job.

CHAPTER 27

OFF-SEASON TRAINING (Be stronger and ski better.)

The purpose of the section is to share with you the many possibilities for off-snow training. It is not our goal to provide you will a detailed exercise program. It is our goal to give you a wide range of fun exercise alternatives that perhaps you have not considered for your workout routines. We have engaged in many of these fun ways to get in shape, and we hope you will be excited to learn about the variety of activities available that are inexpensive, provide excellent results, and in most cases; require only a minimum amount of specialized equipment.

Many people think it is possible to ski themselves into shape when the season starts. But the truth is most skiers can barely finish an easy day on the slopes, and their risk of injury is higher because they are out of shape. With a lot of effort, you may eventually ski yourself into shape about the time April rolls around. With that in mind, we have put together a few exercises and activities you can focus on during the off-season to get ready to ski. Our intention is to excite you about the wide range of possibilities, after which you can design your own program.

A word of caution before we start; the exercises and training activities we will be discussing here are intended for healthy adults, and our intentions are only to give you information. You should always consult a doctor or fitness specialist before you begin any new exercise or activity.

In order to engage in a complete training program for skiing, **you need to combine balance, strength, and aerobic training.** To prepare for your fitness journey there are a few decisions you need to make regarding your commitment. Decide how much time you can allocate to fitness without completely disrupting your everyday life. Lay out some attainable goals in combination with a healthy diet plan that will accompany your march to fitness. Then, prepare yourself mentally by committing to a slow ramp up and methodical progression to fitness through habit formation. *New habits typically take a minimum of thirty days to develop*, and then seem to magically become part of your everyday life.

Deciding how much time you need is dependent on how fit you want to become, and the amount of time you are willing to spend. In the beginning a basic conditioning regimen will require a commitment of about thirty

204

minutes, three times a week. Let's face it; if you put in less time than that you probably won't see significant improvement in your skiing endurance and enjoyment. Once you become comfortable with your basic conditioning routine you may want to increase your workout duration to forty five minutes per time, and increase your total days per week to five. If you exercise five days every week, consider doing strength and balance exercises two days a week and cardiovascular exercises three days a week. For example, you can schedule your strength and balance days on Tuesdays and Thursdays, with your cardiovascular workouts falling on Mondays, Wednesdays, and Fridays.

For some, even our recommendation for the beginning program may be too much, and we do not pretend to know what exercise program is best for any individual. Use common sense to develop your workout schedule and do your homework. It is best to consult a certified strength and conditioning specialist. You can make your quest for fitness as simple or as complicated as you like, but just make sure you get professional guidance before you begin. If you have not been active recently, plan on a minimum of six to twelve weeks to prepare for skiing.

In this book we have talked frequently about loading your skis with energy to initiate turns; although, until now we have not talked about the strength and endurance it takes to do it repeatedly. To get in shape for a great day of skiing, you will need to divide your workout time between activities that improve balance, build strength, and increase stamina. Oh, and it should be fun!

Balance Training

Throughout the book, we have talked about being centered over your skis. To do it, your center of gravity (core) must constantly change position to stay in balance over your skis. If you are not centered you will be habitually adjusting your body position as you endlessly fight to regain your balance. Coincidently, the more you improve your balance the easier it becomes to remain centered over your skis. As a person's balance improves, their body learns to quickly and automatically make the movements that are necessary to stay centered.

Simply put, having great balance is a key requirement if you are going to be an advanced skier, and acquiring improved balance can be fun. To this end we have assembled a list of entertaining activities to improve your workouts and accelerate this process. Some of these may be familiar to you while others may not.

Basic Balance Enhancing Activities
1) Balance Board (fig. 27.1)
2) Linking Short Radius Turns on a Mountain Bike (See fig. 27.2)
3) BOSU® Balance Trainer (fig. 27.3)
4) Balance Beam
5) Indoor Climbing at a Gym

Figure 27.1 *Ski Stance Simulation Exercise on a Balance Board. To start, relax and place arms in the beach ball position, then flex ankles, next center hips over feet, followed by rounding out the lower back, and last, tip upper body slightly forward while relaxing shoulders. When movements are completed correctly, in the above sequence, the balance board will remain level without the edges touching the floor. If the leg muscles are flexing to hold the position, stand up until the legs are able to relax.*

Advanced Balance Enhancing Activities

1) Linking Short Radius Turns on In-Line Skates
2) Exercise Ball (balance up on the ball while exercising)
3) Slack Line (Climber's webbing that is stretched between two fixed anchors or trees. To improve balance, you walk across the webbing that is suspended just above the ground.

   Both the basic and advanced balancing activities should not be attempted without professional instruction. This helps ensure your safety, and you will benefit more quickly from using theses devices correctly.

Figure 27.2 *Linking Short-Radius Turns on a Mountain Bike: On a grassy area, set up a series of cones at 9-12 foot intervals. Use outside-leg dominance with an erect upper body to stay in balance over the outside pedal through each turn. This mimics outside-leg dominant skiing. Just like in skiing, the body mass (CORE) is falling to the inside of the turn. (See above arrow; refer to figure 10.4, and pages 77-78.)*

It is not important which activities you choose to improve your balance; however, it is very important that you apply a relaxed approach to your balance training. Do not become rigid and fight your body's attempts to balance. If you are struggling when practicing balancing exercises, try to feel what your body is doing, and specifically which muscles are tense. Relax these muscles, breath normally, and start again. But, this time approach the same challenge while remaining relaxed. Don't try to force your way to success; be fluid and relax your way into being balanced.

Figure 27.3 BOSU® Balance Trainer: a great tool for building core strength, enhancing balance, and having fun. There are many exercise routines and movements that have been developed for the BOSU® Balance Trainer. Check it out!

Strength Training

Strength conditioning is achieved primarily through floor exercises, weight training, and load bearing activities for your muscles. To start a basic program you can focus your training on developing your legs, upper body, and core.

Having a strong body will help your skiing in many ways. Building strength helps you avoid injuries, sore muscles, and back pain, while adding explosive power and foot-to-foot quickness to your skiing. The following is a suggested list of skiing exercises that will help you build strength. Your local fitness specialist can help you learn these ski specific exercises.

Legs
1) Lunges
2) Squats (butt moves back, knees should not move forward past toes, heels stay on ground)
3) Squat Jumps up Hills or Steps
4) One Legged Squats
5) Lateral Jumps for Strengthening Legs
6) Wall Sits
7) Curls and Extensions for Hamstrings and Quadriceps
8) Slide Board Workout
9) Single-Leg Press with Fitness Ball (designed for two people)
10) Single-Leg Knee Bend

Upper Body
1) Push Ups
2) Pull Ups
3) Pull Downs

Body Core
1) Bridge Exercise
2) Abdominal crunch or sit-up
3) Side Plank
4) Exercise Ball Routines for Core Development
5) Pilates

More detailed information on many of these exercises can be found on the internet.

For us, the best all-around low impact training is indoor climbing. Working out at an indoor climbing gym helps develop almost every muscle in your body, and for the most part, it is a safe activity. But, as in any muscle conditioning workout, you can strain things. If you climb at an indoor gym 2 or 3 days a week, for at least an hour each time, you will become considerably stronger than you are now. This is also a great way to improve your balance, while increasing flexibility.

Stamina

Are your muscles ready for a repetitive motion drill that lasts all day? Most people's muscles fatigue long before a full day of skiing, unless they have worked on their aerobic endurance. When working on endurance training, we like to mix it up by using different methods of exercising during the same week. For instance, we might ride our road bikes on Monday, go for a mountain hike on Wednesday, and ride our mountain bikes on Friday. This kind of cross training keeps it interesting and helps us stay enthusiastic. It's an approach to endurance training that engages you in a wide range of skill building exercises, which is much better than doing the same old thing all the time. This type of training is less structured, but rewards you just the same, and still can lead you to a strong season of skiing.

If I have been unable to train for some time, I start with an easy goal to get back into the swing of lengthy endurance training sessions. I may start with a casual 30 minute road bike ride and note the distance traveled in a log book. Then, each time I do this particular ride my goal is to go further than I did during the last ride. If I have improved my distance for three or four consecutive rides, it is time to increase my ride time and start the process all over again. My mid-term goal is to increase my time and distance, with my long-term goal being a one hour ride. If you are doing endurance training vigorously for one hour, three or four days per week, you will become reasonably fit. Add two days of strength training and some balance work every week, and you will be very fit after two to three months.

It is important to arrange your schedule so that your aerobic workouts fall on the days directly after you do strength building. Strength training increases the amount of lactic acid in your muscles and exercises such as running, swimming, biking, or any other form of aerobic exercise will help flush the acid from your muscles.

Regardless of where you live, the following list gives you many options for endurance training.

1) Mountain Biking
2) In-Line Skating
3) Road Biking
4) Ice Skating
5) Mountain Running
6) Urban Running
7) Stair Running
8) Hiking
9) Hiking w/ a heavy pack (start light and add weight)

10) Roller Skating
11) Swimming
12) Jumping Rope, Jumping Rope while Running
13) Sculling or Rowing
14) Lake Kayaking (different from rowing)

I am a believer in getting out of the gym to get in shape. If you do outdoor activities, it is much easier for you to receive a great workout. When doing outdoor activities, most of these endeavors will include an informal goal. For example, the goal may be to ride your mountain bike on the loop around the park or lake. In these situations you can't quit just because you don't feel like riding, or you won't be going home anytime soon. The implied goal is the ride around the lake, and it is almost impossible not to finish, (unless you call for a sag wagon rescue). Another great way to exercise is by joining group runs or rides, or just finding a partner that pushes your limits a bit. Finally, always measure your progress in any of these activities. If you measure it, improvement will follow!

CHAPTER 28

DIET, THE MOUNTAIN MENU

I will make this short and sweet. Eating right, avoiding alcohol, and drinking water are three more pieces of the puzzle needed to complete the picture of the advanced skier.

I am sure that previous paragraph may upset some people, for as we all know a big part of the ski experience is purported to be après skiing, followed by late night dinner and carousing. Add high altitude and a late night hot tub to this mix of activities and you have a recipe for disaster on skis the following day. Assuming some people are not going to avoid alcohol and rich foods, I would like to lay out a few guide lines for mitigating these influences on your next day of skiing.

After a long day on the slopes your body is dehydrated, and needs fluids. Add to this alcohol consumption and you will probably feel pretty worthless the next day. This can be avoided to some extent by consuming water during the day, right after skiing, and throughout the evening. According to a recommendation from the Institute of Medicine in Washington, D.C., men should consume 3.7 liters of total water per day, and women need 2.7 liters of total water every day. It is important to note that you get water from other sources than just drinking it, so consult your dietitian or doctor to determine how much straight water you should consume daily.

It is estimated that about 90% of the population consumes less than the recommended daily amount, mainly by drinking water only when thirsty. Thirst is not always a reliable way to judge your need for water. It is presumed by the medical community that thirst develops after your body fluids are depleted and you are already functioning at a less than optimal level. Two advantages you can gain from good hydration habits are enhanced mental clarity and an increased energy level, both of which are important for good skiing.

Generally speaking, in order to enjoy a healthy diet that compliments your exercise regimen, you should eat fruits and vegetables while avoiding alcohol, desserts, non-diet soda, and sweetened coffee most of the time. Eating certain red meats, chicken breasts, and most fish (not fried) can be done anytime. There are many diet and exercise books available that will give you specific information on which foods to avoid, and a list of those foods you can eat on a regular basis.

Other things to consider: Eat a healthy breakfast, avoid late night eating, have a healthy snack immediately after skiing, and avoid eating a big dinner. When talking about large meals, remember an average serving size of meat is about 3 to 4 ounces, or just about the same size as a deck of cards. If you are so inclined, a glass of wine is fine at dinner time, but heavy alcohol consumption will only diminish your ability to ski well. A friend of ours said it succinctly; "You can ski, or you can drink." Of course, he was talking about alcohol.

In the area of nutrition, considerable scientific resources have been allocated to determining the make-up of a healthy diet, and the majority of these resources (to the best of my knowledge) do not endorse any short-term or fad diets as a way to live a healthy life style. Earlier, we talked about how exercise routines become habitual after approximately 30 days of repetition. The same holds true for changes in your dietary habits. We suggest you avoid all the diets that claim you can see tremendous results quickly with little or no effort, and that you consult a nutritional expert, dietitian, or doctor to begin your transition to a dietary change and healthy lifestyle. A healthy diet combined with a regular exercise program will make you a better skier.

CHAPTER 29

SKIING UNFAMILIAR RESORTS

When you travel to unfamiliar resorts, there are a few things to consider before you step into your skis and head aimlessly and blissfully (at least in the beginning) out to the lifts. You may be facing a new set of challenges that can have a less than positive outcome on your skiing.

The first of which is altitude. If you are traveling to the Alps or the Rocky Mountains for the first time, and especially Colorado, you will probably be skiing at a much higher elevation than usual. Our secret to dealing with higher altitudes is to slow down, drink more fluids, get a good night's sleep, and (if possible) arrive one day early in order to become more accustomed to the thin air and recover from jet lag or long hours in a car. This can be your shopping day.

Pacing yourself at altitude is a wise decision. Start the ski day with easy warm-up runs, and generally try to take a more relaxed approach to your skiing. If you plan to take on a more difficult section of the mountain, or to ski a popular off-piste run that you must hike to, delay these efforts until you have been at the area for two days if possible. This will give your body time to acclimate as you go to higher altitudes during the day, and then sleep at a lower altitude during the night. In most cases, you will benefit from easy skiing the first two days, and then you can increase your activity level for the rest of your vacation.

Once at the mountain, inquire at the information desk about going on a guided mountain tour led by host skiers. This is the fastest way to get to know the mountain, and discover some of the local's favorite runs or powder caches. A mountain host can also tell you what lifts to avoid right after lunch, where the best on-mountain restaurants are located, the names of the Après skiing hot spots, and most important of all; where to find the best snow. In addition, you should study the area map, and spend a few minutes to develop a basic understanding of the mountain's layout.

One final thought; before you leave home do a quick inspection of your equipment. Start by inspecting your ski bases for gouges or edge damage, and if necessary take this opportunity to have your skis tuned. However, wait until you arrive at the resort to have your skis waxed for the current conditions. Next, look at your boots and be sure to inspect them for broken buckles and cracks in the plastic. Lastly, check out your poles, making sure you have no cuts on the shafts. A significant cut into the shaft of a composite pole could cause it to break.

If you are flying to a destination resort, versus driving, you need not bring your skis or poles. If is much easier to rent skis and poles when you arrive. This assures you receive skis that have been freshly tuned and are ready to go. It can help to know the tip, tail, and waist dimensions of your current skis, along with the name and model, so that you can rent a similar ski. If you feel the rental ski just isn't working for you, simply return them and get a different model of ski. Always bring your boots from home.

S. Phipps Airing it out in the Trees at Rendezvous Mountain near Jackson Hole, Wyoming.

CHAPTER 30

SKIING IN EUROPE (The cost will surprise you.)

If you live in the United States, skiing Europe can be less expensive than spending the same amount of time enjoying one of the fabulous North American resorts. You can also do it without checking any luggage. We know because we have traveled this way, while remaining fashionably dressed (sort of).

To enjoy a low cost ski vacation in Europe, you need to pick one of the lesser known resort areas, but believe me, these can still be amazing resorts on a huge scale when compared to U.S. ski areas. A favorite of mine is the Monte Rosa area in the Italian Alps. From one little village you can access three connected ski areas, comprised of 35 lifts and 18 on-mountain restaurants. It is still a local's area and sees little visitation from people living outside of Europe. However, after the 2006 Winter Olympics that is changing, so get there soon. Now, be forewarned; this region may not be your cup of tea as the night life is virtually non-existent, shopping is limited, and it is relatively remote. On the up side, the people are extremely friendly, the local food and wine is delicious, and the skiing is mind boggling. The Monte Rosa area provides spectacular views of the Alps, including the Matterhorn.

In the winter of 2006 we left home and headed for the Alps, carrying only a small backpack and one other small bag with a shoulder strap. Our ski vacation lasted 16 days, yet we did not check any luggage. Our attire consisted of jeans and upper garments made of hi-tech fabric that could be used for skiing and casual, everyday dress. We all wore our ski jackets, and our small carry-on bags held our ski boots (never leave home without them). The backpacks had our clothing, helmets (filled with underwear), and goggles. You will need to stuff your gloves and other essentials in your boots. I also took a break-down boot dryer, cell phone, ski tuning kit, and a journal to write in. What else do you need? We skied at six resorts and we always had everything we needed. It is such a freeing experience to travel without checking your baggage, and adds to the convenience of using local transportation to get around the different countries. We never rented cars, and only took taxis when absolutely necessary. Using the local transportation is easy, and at the most only requires you know a few sayings in the local language. Where is the train or bus station? Where do I buy tickets? Do you speak English?

English is quickly becoming the universal language of Europe, and every time we go, it seems many more people speak it than when we lasted visited the continent. But, just in case, you should also know how to order food, beer, and wine. Being able to ask for the location of nearest water closet is important.

The Matterhorn, from Zermatt, with Chairlift in Foreground.

Other essentials include phrase books, footwear with removable insoles, and perhaps a metric conversion chart. To make sure I haven't forgotten any other important points, I have created the following list of thoughts on traveling to Europe on a ski vacation. It is the last list in the book, and I hope it will be useful to you.

1) You will be renting your skis, so know the type of ski you prefer and the tip, tail, and waist measurements of your skis you left at home.

2) Write down your DIN settings from the heel and toe pieces of your bindings. The DIN setting is usually a number between 1 and 12 that indicates the release force necessary to release you from the binding before you are injured.

3) Know your weight in kilograms, you pole length in centimeters, and your ski length in centimeters.

4) Check your rental skis before you leave the shop. If they are not tuned and waxed, demand another pair or go to another shop.

5) Avoid Randonnee (Alpine Touring) bindings unless you know what they are and have used them before.

6) At ski areas in Europe you are responsible for your own well-being.

7) Once off-piste, but still in bounds, cliffs and obstacles are not marked, and you are on your own. If you get hurt you will probably have no legal recourse, even if you think the area was at fault.

8) Never explore off-piste terrain without a guide. Guide fees in Europe are relatively inexpensive for a day, and the experience is well worth it.

9) Stay at nearby apartments. Your can reserve them over the internet, but do your homework to assure you find a unit that is clean, reasonably priced, and in the right location as it relates to ski shuttles and buses.

10) Most of the countries with ski areas in the Alps have transportation systems that work great and are very inexpensive.

11) In the Alps, there is a saying about extreme off-piste skiing: You only fall once.

12) Many times you will not be required to sign any kind of liability release to heli-ski or go off-piste with a guide. But, by the same token, the guide will not baby sit you. You can get hurt or die while skiing off-piste in Europe. The guides typically will ski a day with you on-piste, before they agree to take you off-trail. Don't go with guides that do not offer this skill assessment day.

13) Be in excellent physical shape before you arrive at a European ski resort. Many are at high altitudes, and the vertical rise of the resorts in the Alps is far greater than in America. You can expect a single run to exceed five or six thousand vertical feet. That can be as much as five times longer than the average run

in the United States. This is no big deal unless you are at the top of the mountain when it is time to make the last run of the day. Instead of one tiring run, you will be facing the equivalent of four or five runs to finish the day.

14) Do research on local customs. For instance, in Italy, restaurants and shops are rarely open from 12:00 to 2:00 each afternoon. This is especially true in the smaller villages, and we found that in Gressoney Saint Jean some shops rotated the days they were open. You can not always depend on everything being open Monday through Friday.

15) Mailing letters and postcards can be tricky. The main difficulty will be determining the correct amount of postage for each.

16) Mostly, wine by the carafe is very tasty, making it possible to spread out your purchases of wine by the bottle.

17) Ski smart. When off-piste in the Alps, it is very easy to get trapped by dead-end canyons and cliffs after skiing several thousand vertical feet. The walk back up can be difficult and long.

18) Expect to have a fabulous time skiing in Europe, and the more planning and research you do before you go will pay huge dividends toward the enjoyment of the trip. Going with friends that speak the language of your host country is a big plus.

19) Off-Piste = Off the Groomed Runs.

For information on upcoming Weekend Warrior's Guides go to:

www.weekendwarriorsguide.com

Israel poses with Lo Stambecco: **This majestic animal is the mountain goat of the Maritime Alps.**

NOTES: